Whither Globalization?

The vortex of knowledge and ideology

James H. Mittelman

Routledge
Taylor & Francis Group

LONDON AND NEW YORK

First published 2004 by Routledge
11 New Fetter Lane, London EC4P 4EE

Simultaneously published in the USA and Canada
by Routledge
29 West 35th Street, New York, NY 10001

Routledge is an imprint of the Taylor & Francis Group

© 2004 James H. Mittelman

Typeset in Baskerville by Steven Gardiner Ltd, Cambridge
Printed and bound in Great Britain by
TJ International Ltd, Padstow, Cornwall

British Library Cataloguing in Publication Data
A catalogue record for this book is available from the British Library

Library of Congress Cataloging in Publication Data
A catalog record for this book has been requested

ISBN 0-415-34206-6 (hbk)
ISBN 0-415-34152-3 (pbk)

Whither Globalization?

'A thorough assessment of globalization studies and a probing examination of the links between knowledge, ideology and power in contemporary globalization. Very timely and well recommended.'

Jan Aart Scholte, Professor and Acting Director,
Centre for the Study of Globalisation and Regionalisation, University of Warwick

'Mittelman addresses a crucial yet understudied feature of the current period: the ways in which globalization alters the balance between a dominant US-driven paradigm and the multiple forms of local knowledge that continue to be a presence around the world. He shows how this particular form of intellectual and ideological dominance creates in turn the conditions for the emergence of countervailing representations and contestatory types of knowledge. His is a major contribution to the scholarship on globalization.'

Saskia Sassen, Ralph Lewis Professor of Sociology, University of Chicago

'Speaking from his experiences in multiple global venues, Mittelman has written a visionary text, sure to appeal to neophytes and gurus alike.'

Michael Burawoy, Goldman Distinguished Professor in the Social Sciences,
University of California, Berkeley, and President of the American Sociological Association

Globalization is usually said to be about markets, power, and culture. *Whither Globalization?* goes further, arguing that globalization may also be understood as a way of knowing and representing the world. Mittelman debunks prevalent myths about globalization and 'anti-globalization', presenting 'alterglobalization' as another force and indicating the prospects for a new common sense about world order. Drawing on original field research in Japan and the United States, this book shows how globalization itself and globalization studies have changed since 9/11. Compact and accessible, *Whither Globalization?* is a major statement by one of the leading scholars in the field and is essential reading for students in the social sciences, especially international studies and international political economy.

Key content includes:

Part I	Power	
Part II	Knowledge	
Part III	Ideology	
Part IV	Transformative possibilities	

James H. Mittelman is Professor of International Relations in the School of International Service at American University, Washington, DC.

Rethinking globalizations
Edited by Barry K. Gills
University of Newcastle upon Tyne, in connection with the Globalization Research Network

This series is designed to break new ground in the literature on globalization and its academic and popular understanding. Rather than perpetuating or simply reacting to the economistic understanding of globalization, this series seeks to capture the term and broaden its meaning to encompass a wide range of issues and disciplines and convey a sense of alternative possibilities for the future.

The tone of the series will be problem-oriented, practical and accessible; assuming the role of the public intellectual as well as the specialized academic. It will seek to identify a set of global problems and address these in a way that allows readers to receive needed and essential information, as well as encounter new ideas about practical solutions and alternatives.

**For Linda,
Alexandra, Jordan, and Alicia**

Contents

PART IV
Transformative possibilities   87

Tables

Preface and acknowledgments

The front cover of this book shows an owl perched on a globe marked by meridians, not borders, and encompassed by a vortex of globally iconic ideas. These themes may be traced to ancient Greek and Roman civilizations, in which the owl signified knowledge and wisdom. In those times, the goddesses Athena and Minerva were often accompanied by the owl, an emblem for identifying deities. With Roman conquest, the mythologies and their symbolic representations spread to other parts of the world. The knowledge of antiquity and its images melded with imperial force as a means to establish and maintain empire. Hence Athena sometimes appeared in full armor, and Minerva was also the divinity of war.

But there are other stories. Just as the owl portrays knowledge in the dominant order, it assumes darker meanings in images formed at the margins of global power. For example, in the mythologies and religions of China, Japan, India, Egypt, and Mexico, the owl betokens death, night, and coldness. So, too, these non-Western civilizations have produced their own sciences, understandings, and signatures. Throughout the world, markings of identification, such as the crescent and star of Islam, the spear and shield of liberation brandished by the African National Congress, the cross of Christianity, La Marianne embodying the values of republicanism, and the hammer and sickle for communism, have all been drawn into figurative and actual combat.

Two millennia after the apex of the Hellenic–Roman period, power holders have greater prowess and scientific advancements have been astounding. Old logos co-exist with contemporary ideas and their pennants, including a fist (black power), a tree (environmentalism), the swoosh (Nike, the name of the winged goddess of victory in Greek mythology), and the mask covering a face (Zapatistas). This multifaceted imagery points to fundamental issues about the knowledge claims and ideological representations inscribed in the structure of global power.

Beginning with Francis Bacon's dictum that 'knowledge is power', twentieth-century theorists, such as Max Weber, Antonio Gramsci, Michel Foucault, Edward Said, and successor social constructivists, advanced understanding of this link.[1] While it would take us too far afield to systematically present each author's work and their often diverging perspectives, together they showed that power is rarely exercised without some type of cognitive support and symbolic legitimacy. Indeed, the production of subjectivity cannot be studied alone or treated as merely a scholastic matter. Knowledge and the ways in which political and material processes are represented are not independent of power relations, as the idealism of certain philosophers would have it. Building on this foundation of critical inquiry, I want to examine knowledge and ideology as they pivot on the power of globalization in the twenty-first century.

This book probes contemporary globalization, delimited from the 1970s, though there are of course continuities and discontinuities with previous eras. Within this period, there are different vectors, the main ones studied here being neoliberal globalization and alterglobalization, terms explored more fully in the ensuing chapters.

To the extent that contemporary globalization is as an ascendant paradigm, it constitutes powerful processes of knowledge production and ideological formation. Inasmuch as scholarship is increasingly globalized, intellectual innovation involves the dissemination of US social science around the world and changes the balance between dominant paradigms and local knowledge. Just as the global power structure is institutionalized, so do a knowledge system and dominant ideological representations both constrain and open possibilities for the emergence of alternatives.

That said, my point is that the power of globalization transforms the ways in which knowledge is produced and spawns ideologies. I contend that *globalization is becoming a form of intellectual power embodied in a knowledge system, propagated by institutionalized authority, and manifested in neoliberal ideology*. However, in a dialectical manner, intellectual resistance in the academic and everyday worlds is giving rise to *alterglobalization*: an ensemble of countervailing power, competing knowledge sets, and ideological contestation.

Major questions follow and guide this inquiry. How to conceptualize the ways in which globalization is powering knowledge systems and ideology? What are the evolving knowledge systems and ideological forms employed to reconstitute structures of global power? On the basis of historical tendencies and embodied practices, what kinds of alterglobalization can be projected?

In answering these questions, I will try to pull back the curtain on a series of relationships that are either hidden or denied. This book is primarily concerned with the ways in which powerful globalizing forces shape the subjectivity of their agents, as well as the counterpoints to this structure. The aim here is to offer both a critical analysis of the subjective dimensions of globalization and a future-oriented approach.

My interest in this topic originated more than three decades ago when I was a student at Makerere University in Uganda and, subsequently, a 'special tutor' (junior faculty member) there. This experience opened worlds to me. I have never recovered. There, I carried out research for my dissertation and what became my first book, *Ideology and Politics in Uganda: From Obote to Amin*. Now, I am picking up on this theme in a broader and hopefully more penetrating way.

This endeavor was spurred by Barry Gills's kind invitation to write the inaugural volume in his book series *Globalizations*. It has been a privilege to work again with Craig Fowlie, my editor at Routledge.

One of my principal debts is to my students at American University in Washington, DC, and Ritsumeikan University in Kyoto. They prodded me, criticized my initial formulations, and carried out parts of this research. Special thanks go to my research assistants, some of whose contributions are cited in the Notes that appear at the end of the book. Priya Dixit provided stellar help and offered many excellent suggestions that contributed importantly to this volume. Also, Glenn Adler, my co-author in Chapter 6, more than held up his end of the bargain. In preparing this book, I have also benefited from the advice of Robert Denemark, Björn Hettne, Patrick Jackson, Stephen Rosow, and Paul Wapner. Richard Falk and James Rosenau's encouragement has been extremely valuable. A long conversation that began in 1972 with Robert W. and Jessie Cox and their friendship have strengthened my work and offered many pleasurable moments. Most important, Linda Yarr is my foremost intellectual partner and constructive critic. For that, I am deeply indebted.

Some chapters draw on my essays published between 2002 and 2004. As I wrote them, it became increasingly clear that the themes are closely connected. Jointly, they point to a not wholly coherent, but an inchoate and emergent alterglobaliz- ation. These essays are completely revised in this book, supplemented by new ideas and fresh data, and woven together in the text.

I want to thank the following copyright holders for permission to incorporate material in revised form:

Blackwell Publishing: 'Mapping Globalization', *Singapore Journal of Tropical Geography* 22, no. 3 (November 2001): 212–18. 'Globalization: An Ascendant Paradigm?' *International Studies Perspectives* 3, No. 1 (February 2002): 1–14. 'What Is Critical Globalization Studies?' *International Studies Perspectives* 5, No. 3 (August 2004): 219–30.

Institute of Geography and Regional Science, University of Graz, Austria: 'The Power of Globalization', in Friedrich M. Zimmermann and Susanne Janschitz, eds, *Regional Policies in Europe – The Knowledge Age: Managing Global, Regional and Local Interdependencies* (2002), pp. 9–16.

Routledge (Taylor and Francis Books): 'Globalization Debates: Bringing in Micro-encounters', *Globalizations* 1, No. 1 (September 2004), in press. http://www.tandf.co.uk/journals/titles/14747731.asp

Rowman and Littlefield: 'Ideologies and the Globalization Agenda', in Manfred B. Steger, ed., *Rethinking Globalism* (2003), pp. 15–26.

Sage Publications: 'Reconstituting "Common-Sense" Knowledge: Represen- tations of Globalization Protests', *International Relations* 18, No. 2 (June 2004): 189–211.

None of the people or publishers acknowledged above are implicated in the final product, for which I alone am responsible.

Abbreviations

EU	European Union
G-8	Group of Eight
IFI	International Financial Institution
IMF	International Monetary Fund
JCNC	Japan Committee for Negros Campaign
NAFTA	North American Free Trade Agreement
NGO	Nongovernmental Organization
PP21	People's Plan for the Twenty-First Century
TNC	Transnational Corporation
UNDP	United Nations Development Program
WEF	World Economic Forum
WSF	World Social Forum
WTO	World Trade Organization

Part I

Power

Part 1

Power

1   The power of globalization

The primary concern of this book is the subjective framework of globalization, namely, knowledge and ideology.[1] This theme requires considering the dynamics of global power. Indeed, the power of globalization orients the development of dominant knowledge. And knowledge about globalization is, in turn, represented as ideology: a way of interpreting the world and for contemplating strategies of action. Powerful knowledge sets and, as Antonio Gramsci (1971) showed, compelling ideological discourses are fundamental to eliciting consent and lessening reliance on the material and coercive instruments of a hegemonic order. Hence, knowledge and ideology should not be construed as either mechanically reflecting material power conditions or wholly autonomous from them. Rather, there is a series of interactions, best understood as being contingent.

Critical knowledge and counterideologies betray prevailing myths about globalization and challenge the structures that bolster it. In addition, the relationships among the power of globalization, knowledge, and ideology are uneven and contested. Just as globalization is inscribed with social power relations, knowledge and ideology are a vortex of struggle.

Chapter 1 initiates discussion of the key concepts that I intend to build in the pages that follow. It also presents some of the main points to be fleshed out, thus providing a basis for indicating the ways in which the cognitive and ideological aspects of global power operate.

In that much of the early writing on globalization one-sidedly emphasized market-driven phenomena, this chapter serves as a point of entry for revisiting major attempts to come to grips with the concepts of power and globalization. It is also an opportunity to introduce critical formulations and raise new questions. Here, I will argue that if one regards globalization as a complex of processes, it is possible to reveal certain reductive myths. After dispelling these misunderstandings, my objectives are to explore major issues around which the power of globalization manifests, and to probe the counterpoint to contemporary globalization, i.e. alterglobalization.

Concepts

The concepts of power and globalization may be seen from different observation points, each of which provides a lens for viewing these multifaceted phenomena.[2]

Most often, power is understood in an active, overt sense: X makes Y alter behavior. One actor has power over another actor. The notion that power affects people's interests and is linked to resistance becomes explicit in Max Weber's definition of power as 'the probability that one actor within a social relationship will be in a position to carry out his own will despite resistance' (1978: 53). There is also covert power. Whereas X exercises power over Y, the covert process is subtler in that it entails agenda-setting. Adding to this meaning, structural power draws especially on material and normative capabilities, with incentives for compliance. Hence, Niccolò Machiavelli pictured the world as a thoroughly treacherous place in which the qualities most useful to a prince, or that a prince should appear to have, are likened to a centaur: half-man, half-beast. Both require a capacity to comprehend how to employ them:

> Thus, you must know that there are two kinds of combat: one with laws, the other with force. The first is proper to man, the second to beasts; but because the first is often not enough, one must have recourse to the second.
>
> (Machiavelli 1985: 69)

This is a matter of determining what are the positions of authority and which prince – collective agency writ large – will hold them.

In yet another sense, there is repressive and disciplinary power. The French philosopher Michel Foucault held that dominant power is exercised through social institutions such as medicine, school systems, the barracks, and prison. Power is constituted by discourses, which are strongly bounded areas of knowledge, a complex of statements by which the world is known. In other words, the world is brought into being and relationships are deciphered through the construction of subjectivity: a set of signs and practices that includes rules, many of them unspoken but controlling behavior. For Foucault, power and knowledge are thus joined. He also maintained that discursive power cannot exist without resistance. Power and resistance comprise one another in a contest of opposing strategies for structuring social relationships – an insight to which I will return in Chapters 2 and 7.

Like power, globalization has different meanings. There are three possibilities for conceptualizing it. Simply put, globalization is often understood as an increase in interconnections or growing interdependence on a world scale. Probing further, scholars have defined globalization as a compression of time and space. Speeded by new technologies, events in one part of the world instantly affect what takes place in distant locales. These definitions are helpful as far as they go; however, they are silent about social hierarchies and power relations. Arguably, a more useful avenue of inquiry is to approach globalization as a historical transformation. It is a transformation in the economy in that livelihoods and modes of existence change; in politics, since the locus of power gradually shifts above and below territorial states, forming a multilevel system; and in culture, insofar as there is an erosion of certain life-ways and the emergence of new hybrid forms. Globalization, in turn, engenders both accommodation and resistance. After all, this power structure has an uneven impact on various strata in different regions and countries.

Thesis

That said, globalization is not a single, unified phenomenon. Elsewhere (Mittelman 2000), I have argued that globalization is a *syndrome* of processes and activities: a syndrome in the sense of a pattern of related characteristics, not a pathology, which is the way that the medical profession employs this term to depict symptoms of a disease. Globalization is by no means an abnormality. Rather, it has been normalized as a dominant ideology that joins with neoliberalism to extol the virtues of individualism, efficiency, competition, and minimal state intervention in the economy. Neoliberalism also forms a policy framework, whose instruments of deregulation, liberalization, and privatization center on heightened market integration (Gray 1998).

My earlier book *The Globalization Syndrome* (Mittelman 2000) delimits a series of relationships among the political, economic, and cultural levels. There are interactions but no one-way determinism among these dimensions. To recap my analytical framework, I believe that globalization is a triangulated structure. Not the only factors, three processes stand out: the global division of labor and power, a new regionalism, and resistance politics.

Building on Adam Smith's concept of the division of labor, which centers on specialization in production, a construct later extended by David Ricardo to the realm of trade and by Karl Marx, Max Weber, and Emile Durkheim to other spheres, one might profitably employ this heuristic to explore contemporary globalization, taking care not to privilege the economic side of globalization at the expense of its other dimensions. Going beyond these classical theorists, it is useful to think of the global division of labor *and* power as the anatomy of the global political economy. With globalization, this division has shifted from a near dichotomy between industrialized and industrializing countries to a relocation of production, in which the former have climbed the value-added ladder to more technologically intensive economies while a major share of manufacturing has spread to other parts of the world. The contemporary global division of labor and power is characterized by large-scale flows of capital, technology, and workers among and within regions. These flows are facilitated by the emergence of transnational cultural structures – for example, a Chinese division of labor stretching from East and Southeast Asia to Europe and the Americas – that lubricate the machinery of big, impersonal processes.

The emergent global division of labor and power is refracted by a new regionalism, as with the European Union (EU). The new regionalism is comprised of both formal institutions and informal processes, solidarities rooted in economy and culture, as in cross-border processes in Africa, where territorial lines were imposed by colonial powers, often without regard for natural frontiers demarcated by rivers and mountains or ethnic distribution. Clearly, the global division of labor and power articulates differently with bottom-up institutions, such as civil societies, in different locales. If so, and despite the wiring of social relations in distant locations into networks, place remains salient, albeit of changing significance.

In different parts of the world, the power component of the global division of labor has a counterpoint, for it provokes resistance politics. Resistance to neoliberal globalization, which promotes greater market integration, is of two kinds. It may be open and publicly declared, as at the 'Battle of Seattle', followed by large demonstrations at meetings of major holders of political and economic power in Washington, Prague, Melbourne, Seoul, Quebec City, Genoa, and other cities. Or resistance may be more subtle, latent, and expressed in everyday life. It is apparent, for example, in consumer choices such as antipathy for or reluctance to purchase certain imported products, as well as humor evident in cartoons and popular writing, including novels and plays. Both types of resistance precipitate a search for alternatives to the contemporary form of neoliberal globalization. Integral to this search is a widespread realization that globalization offers many benefits *as well as* a price for integrating in this framework and adopting its practices.

Myths

The argument pursued in *The Globalization Syndrome* can be taken further by focusing on arch myths about globalization: traps and confusions on the route to the intersection between power and globalization. Important here are categories of analysis and language – the very vocabulary used to discuss globalization – which bear directly on thought patterns implicated in the exercise of power.

Integral to much popular and scholarly writing on globalization are categories of analysis that predate the contemporary globalization period. Without reflection on this matter, it is generally assumed that they can be carried over and applied to the current phase of globalization. However, globalizing processes, such as the criminalization of the state in some parts of the world and the privatization of erstwhile public activities, shed new light on categories like legality and the public sphere, which are deeply ingrained in social thought and represented in the media. Strikingly, many of them are binary categories rendered antiquated by globalization. If so, globalization calls for intellectual innovation and new ways of understanding. In addition, the pedagogical implications are far-reaching.

Insofar as the power of globalization is addressed by the schools and in public, the coverage embraces prevalent myths. One is the notion that we live in a 'global village'. This pithy phrase helps to direct attention to the compression of time and space, discussed above, but is misleading in that it clouds increasing discrepancies between the winners and losers in contemporary restructuring. It is not that everyone is coming together in a single worldwide community; rather, certain zones, notably much of Africa and enclaves elsewhere, some of them in the wealthiest countries, are marginalized from the central mechanisms of political and economic globalization. These zones and enclaves have been excluded from the so-called global village. What is more, globalizing processes are destroying scores of villages. Increasingly, small producers are being drawn into a globalizing economy – for instance, in export processing zones in their home countries and by opportunities for work overseas – a process that tears at indigenous social structures, is associated with the spread of AIDS, and wipes out the most productive segments of the population in many villages. In fact, some of the villages in Uganda, where I stayed as a student at Makerere University, Kampala, are now ghost towns. The social structures are no longer intact, and the villagers are almost entirely the elderly and young children, many of them orphans – a phenomenon practically unknown in the days when the extended family was expected to, and could, provide a safety net.

Another myth, then, is that globalization homogenizes conditions throughout the world. True, there is much standardization, as with consumer products. Some of them are world products such as automobiles, reflecting cross-border mergers and the parceling out of production processes, as well as design and assembly, to different countries. At the same time, greater diversity is emerging in the form of new hybrids of the global and the local. Take the English language, often considered to be a key agent in the spread of globalization. Actually, actors in various locales are appropriating English and creating novel forms of speech, as with Singlish in Singapore.

By the same token, it is wrong to subscribe to the myth that globalization and Americanization are one and the same. Yes, the US has probably benefited more from globalization than any other country. Globalization is surely heavily American. But not all global products are American forms. Consider reggae music, the croissant, and Japanese animation. How many young Americans, Europeans, and Asians of different nationalities are growing up watching not Bugs Bunny or Mickey Mouse but Japanese cartoons from Doraemon to Dragon Ball and Crayon Shinchan? Also, like other parts of the world, mid-America is experiencing the shocks of globalization, as formerly tightly knit neighborhoods absorb new waves of immigration and the job market changes, to a certain degree prompted by plant closings in favor of cheap labor overseas.

These patterns should not be construed as what the mythology presents as a move toward a 'borderless world'. Although European countries have established a European passport and facilitated the movement of citizens across borders, it is the state that grants citizenship and restrains or eases migration. Even if certain global flows, such as knowledge and information on the Internet, easily transcend national borders, the principle of territoriality still matters. Territorially based sovereignty has not disappeared, but must be seen in conjunction with other principles of social organization. They co-exist in an emergent multilevel world order, subject to increasing contestation.

Contrary to what is frequently alleged, globalization is thus neither inevitable nor irresistible. There is no juggernaut of expanding markets and technological forces powering history to a forgone conclusion. Rather, if globalization has been made by humankind, then it can be unmade or remade by humans. History is open-ended, not foreordained. The resistance apparent in Seattle and other venues of protest over globalization is emblematic of fledgling efforts to reshape neoliberal globalization.

The idiom 'antiglobalization', which has become commonplace in the media and popular writing, warrants scrutiny, for it is vague and used promiscuously. More than a quibble over terminology, it should be clearly stated that the trope 'antiglobalization', now in vogue, constitutes an intersubjective image engraved in the structure of power. By slotting a wide variety of stances on globalization in two boxes – for and against – it obscures the varied complaints about globalizing trends that have emerged from different locales and diverse points on the political spectrum. What becomes obscure are the varied attempts to engage – not evade – globalization. In fact, most of the resistance is *against* neoliberalism and *for* globalization such that it should serve social ends. In this sense, the resistance is neither *anti*globalization nor *pro*globalization.

Applied to head-on confrontations – such as the Group of Eight (G-8) meeting at Genoa in 2001, which culminated in violent clashes with police and the death of a protestor – the label 'antiglobalization' fails to capture crucial distinctions on the spectrum from reformist to nonreformist positions. Some protestors advanced proposals for adjustments in international institutions, especially the World Trade Organization (WTO), the International Monetary Fund (IMF), and the World Bank, while other activists (not only on the Left, but also proponents of free trade) advocated abolishing the institutions themselves. There were efforts to change the direction and content of policy, and intentions to transform the underlying structures. Indeed, it is important to distinguish along a continuum between those against neoliberal globalization but not capitalism, and those against capitalism itself, with globalization deemed to be the current phase.

The point is that the prevalent imagery of 'antiglobalization' is problematic since it defines a phenomenon solely as a negation. It impoverishes social criticism by mystifying what may be learned from the debates over globalization without regard for what may be positive and affirmative. At the venues where public protests against neoliberal globalization have taken place, varied social movements have raised important issues about the underside of globalization, including the relationship between increasing market power and political authority, a matter that worries not only groups within civil society but also the holders of state power.

Indeed, when the Asian financial crisis, also called economic crisis, struck Malaysia in 1997 and, within a few weeks, resulted in a 40 per cent drop in the value of its currency (the ringgit), equivalent to the economic gains of 40 years of political independence, Prime Minister Mahathir Mohamad complained loudly about currency speculators, but found that there was no international body empowered to act on his complaints. His main adversary in this script, financier George Soros, similarly cautioned that markets, when left to their own devices, do not tend toward equilibrium. Markets, he held, are unstable, and the global system urgently requires a new form of regulation. Also frustrated by the inability to harness globalizing processes, President Fernando Henrique Cardoso candidly stated that he did not rule Brazil, because globalization is swallowing national states. He also lamented that the 'increase in inequality and exclusion that globalization fuels is intricate and difficult to counter' (as quoted in Leite 1996: 25).

Finally, pigeonholing social criticism as antiglobalization hampers the creation of alternatives. Many critics resist not because they are against globalization, but because, without indulging utopian dreams, they are imagining possibilities for a more inclusive, participatory, and democratic globalization. However diverse, they are for alterglobalization when it means *an attempt to reshape globalizing forces so as to mitigate their harms and distribute the opportunities in a just manner.* Although the exact origins of the term alterglobalization are obscure, its usage in French ('alter-mondialisation') dates from the last decade and is on the rise in Europe. The meaning of alterglobalization is difficult to pin down, and subsequent chapters (especially Chapter 8) attempt to explicate this move as well as its variants.

Issues

The main issues around which the power of globalization manifests, then, are the state, global governance, and resistance. Each issue invokes and combines the different frames for viewing globalization noted earlier.

Clearly, the nation-state does not remain passive while the global economy is rapidly changing. The state system is not fixed and invariant: it has been evolving since its inception at Westphalia in 1648. On the one hand, some argue that with the rapid growth of market power, the state is a declining entity, a relic of a bygone era. As Cardoso maintains, the state does not have the power to control large global flows, which, with the click of a mouse, instantly transcend and penetrate national borders. Similarly, critics contend that capital collectively wields the power to discipline the state, as with currency speculators and IMF structural adjustment programs.

An opposing view is that the state has made important policy adjustments to accommodate globalization – for example, the current tendency to embrace reregulation in Latin America. It is claimed that in fact, the state is powering globalization. The state is deemed to be the author of globalization, exemplified by the role that the Clinton Administration, with the active support of the governments of Canada and Mexico, played in the inauguration of the North American Free Trade Agreement (NAFTA) and over the objections of much of the constituency of the Democratic Party – most of organized labor and environmentalists (Panitch 1996).

Yet another interpretation is that the state now acts less as a shield for the domestic economy against the international economy, as it did during the 1960s and 1970s (when some countries nationalized the commanding heights and others similarly placed restrictions on transnational capital). By contrast, it is at present more of a facilitator of domestic economic interests. As argued by Robert Cox (1987: 253–65), it is thereby an agent that promotes globalization. From this perspective, the state is in the throes of restructuring.

Implicit in this debate is the vexing question, who governs globalization? It is sometimes claimed, as did Mahathir during the Asian financial crisis, no one is in charge. The state is caught in a dialectic, subject to increasing pressure from above, market forces and international organizations such as the EU, and from below in the form of demands from civil society. At the same time, there is a marked trend toward informal governance. Increasingly prominent are groups such as the World Economic Forum (WEF, a private foundation that each year brings together CEOs of the one thousand largest corporations in the world, central bankers, presidents, prime ministers, journalists, and some scholars, usually in Davos, Switzerland), the Trilateral Commission, and credit-rating agencies (e.g. Moody's and Standard & Poor's, whose evaluations can make or break developing economies). The tendency is to supplement the more conventional layers of governance with privatized governance, a tendency apparent in the realm of military security, with the proliferation of private militias, self-defense forces, and security firms that provide protection at home, especially when the police are incompetent or so corrupt that they are part of the problem. Private agencies are setting agendas, disseminating neoliberal ideas about increasing integration in the global market, playing a key role in shaping economies, and taking over aspects of national security when the state either willingly or reluctantly relinquishes its supposed monopoly over the legitimate use of force.

With major tensions in the configuration of global power, much of the debate concerns which rules will be adopted, and whose rules these are. For its part, the resistance to neoliberal globalization is incipient and varied. Although it is not a coherent movement, the resistance has succeeded in placing a powerful question on the agenda of the proponents of globalization: if globalization is to become a rule-based system, whose will should prevail in determining the rules? That of massive concentrations of private economic power, national political authorities, civil societies, or some combination of these forces? In all likelihood, the resolution of this matter – no less than the future course of the historical transformation marking this century – will be determined by a mix of disciplinary power and counterpower. The lines between power and counterpower are increasingly fluid and unsettled. Recalling Machiavelli's concept of power as a centaur, evidently the combat will take place through both reason and coercion. To the extent that reason is unable to hold sway, the result is the application of brute force.

Democracy

If one prefers reason to coercion, then it is worth asking, what is the key to avoiding the dark side of globalization? In good measure, this is a matter of normative preferences.

A large part of the problem is that markets are rapidly expanding and lack accountability. Adhering to the logic of the market system, the economically powerful seek to maximize profits and beat their competitors. They are chief beneficiaries of neoliberal globalization, and have no inherent interest in accountability.

Accountability is a core tenet of democracy. In its several variants, democracy is not a final state of affairs but unfolds with changing dynamics. Democracy heretofore has been framed for territorial states that purportedly can contain the movement of people, ideas, and technologies. However, many states, especially the ones with large concentrations of diasporic populations and citizens employed by firms based in other regions, are now subject to pressures for deterritorialization and denationalization. With globalization, democracy must be reterritorialized – strengthened both within and across state borders – as a method of governance for regions and, indeed, for solving global problems. As in the EU, but also on an interregional scale, the challenge then is to rethink the concept of national democracy and bring it in line with a form of politics in which boundaries are not eradicated but blurred or complicated by transborder arrangements.

In this transformation, a vital issue is the matter of access. How can global governance be recast so that the many may participate in the steering and growth mechanisms of the powerful structures that comprise globalization? There cannot be much assurance of the eventual outcome of an open-ended, historical process, but making clear the dynamics, knowing the constraints, and imagining the possibilities mark the direction likely to put humankind on a path toward a just future. It is upon this premise that the ensuing analysis of globalization and alterglobalization is based. Let us now turn to the cognitive dimensions.

Part II

Knowledge

2 Mapping globalization

To come to grips with globalization, one must map it, because, at all times, globalization *takes place* – albeit in intricate and varied ways.[1] As a form of restructuring, with winners and losers, globalization is constituted by resistance, and these processes occur in particular places that have distinctive features – historical trajectories, cultural endowments, local coalitions, and so on. A map of globalization may be drawn by showing the spaces of resistance, many of which are found at the local level, sometimes with transnational links involving formal or informal networks.

Globalization as a loss of control

For many people, a major propellant of resistance is experiencing neoliberal globalization as a loss in the degree of control – for some actors, however little to begin with – exercised locally. There is less control over market forces that transcend the Westphalian, territorial state. The lessening of political control is manifested in the ways in which embodiments of the market – for example, IMF and World Bank structural adjustment programs or capital flight precipitated by currency speculators – discipline the state. Caught in a dialectic, the state, as noted in Chapter 1, is increasingly pressured from above, particularly by market forces and macroregional processes, and from below, especially from civil society and social movements. Moreover, in the face of transnational industries, such as Hollywood, there is an erosion of cultural dignity, though assertions, or reassertions, from below may attempt to counter such trends.

To illustrate the issue of cultural loss in the context of neoliberal globalization, it is important to bear in mind that each language uniquely captures thoughts and that when the words are extinct, the thoughts may disappear as well. If a language dies, aspects of the culture, including a pool of diverse ideas, goes with it. While dominant languages have long come into contact with smaller languages, evidence suggests that the process of killing off the less prevalent languages is accelerating. Hence, according to linguists, it is estimated that more than 50 per cent of the world's 6,000 languages will die out over the next 100 years, and only five per cent remain 'safe' in the sense that they are spoken by at least one million people and are backed by the state (Wurm 1996: 5; 'Cultural Loss Seen as Languages

Fade' 1999). The rate of language extinction varies by region, but in the Peruvian Amazon, early missionaries reported over 500 languages among isolated communities – more conservatively estimated by linguists as 100 to 150 languages, with myriad dialects. Today, only 57 of these languages survive, 25 of them endangered to the point of imminent extinction ('Cultural Loss Seen as Languages Fade' 1999). This loss of heritage may be considered a form of cultural narrowing, but it is also accompanied by increasing diversity. Some countries, such as Canada and in Europe, are debating legal measures to protect national and subnational languages. The growing prominence of English has prompted critics and civil society groups to defend the use of their own languages, which is a matter of identity and values – the question not only of symbols, but also contestation over meanings.

Resistance

In some cases, the defense against neoliberal globalization generates resistance, a construct that must be properly delimited and a phenomenon that should not be romanticized. As a part of contemporary globalization itself, resistance is not mere opposition.

Before the present period of globalization and in other contexts, the heuristic resistance has been employed in various ways. In order to sensitize one to the array of issues that it opens up and to take account of its several dimensions, I will briefly note multiple shades of meaning.

In the natural sciences, resistance is regarded as a property with the power to transform. It is part of a circuit that converts electrical energy into heat in collision with other currents or particles. The resistance of a circuit element or conductor may increase with higher temperatures, or with cooling, may drop to zero. That is, a coil with transformative potential is a resistor. In another sense, resistance refers to the immunity of a body to a disease. It is a protective mechanism regarded by medical researchers as, under different conditions, either a genetic or acquired response to infective, invasive, or foreign agents. Resistance exempts, renders ineffective, and neutralizes infectious organisms (Imam 2001).

Historically, the term resistance is associated with secret and clandestine groups that formed in German-occupied Europe during World War II against Nazi rule. Their ranks encompassed civilians, armed bands of partisans, and guerrilla fighters whose activities included sabotaging enemy operations, providing intelligence information to the Allies, and assisting Jews and others to escape. In other cases, nonviolent – or passive – resistance entails a refusal to obey and efforts to exact concessions. As with civil disobedience, the resistance seeks to set a moral example so as to effect change. Its efficacy thus hinges on an appeal to morality. The philosophy of civil disobedience has its roots in the ancient Greek and Roman traditions, can be traced through Mahatma Gandhi and Martin Luther King Jr., and has standing in international law. For example, at the Nuremberg war crime trials it was declared that under certain circumstances, an individual may be held accountable for failure to break the laws of his or her state, thereby suggesting standards that transcend the territorial space over which a state claims absolute authority (i.e. sovereignty). Additionally, in much feminist theory, resistance signifies more than a reaction, a backlash against, or challenges to, prevalent norms. Rather, resistance takes place in both consciousness and practice. It permits agency and possibilities of alternatives to patriarchy. Put briefly, feminist concepts of resistance include not only critique, but also positive efforts to effect structural transformation (Imam 2001, citing Fisher and Davis 1993; Laslett, Brenner, and Arat 1995; and Cosslett, Easton, and Summerfield 1996).

The work of individual social theorists also stands out, because some writers have done more than others to push the concept of resistance. Certainly, a seminal contribution is Karl Polanyi's notion of the double movement (1957). Tracing the expansion and deepening of the market at the dawn of industrial capitalism during the eighteenth and nineteenth centuries, he showed that the socially disruptive and polarizing effects sparked self-protective measures in the form of countermovements. Whereas Polanyi's analysis focuses on the rise of capitalism in England and its implications, other authors (e.g. Sakamoto 1994) have sought to extend his framework to contemporary market integration. Polanyi's insights are most useful in terms of understanding formal movements, but these are initiatives that have coalesced organizationally. There are others that have not congealed and may be most readily discerned in the cultural realm.

The latter route is taken by Gramsci (1971), whose concept of hegemony may be understood as an amalgam of consent and coercion in which consent is the predominant element. For Gramsci, the institutions of civil society, including the family, schools, the church, the media, and trade unions, give meaning to everyday life so that the need for the application of force is reduced. Hegemony is established when power and control over everyday life are perceived as emanating from self-government (individuals embedded in communities) as much as from external sources such as the state or dominant strata. Hegemony, then, requires the participation of subaltern groups. They may either support a hegemonic project or, in varying degrees, resist it. Counterhegemony may take one of two forms: 'wars of movement' are frontal assaults on the state (e.g. labor strikes and military action), whereas 'wars of position', such as boycotts, impede the functions of the state, are gradual and involve changing attitudes. In both cases, the objective is to seize control of the state. With contemporary globalization, however, the state may or may not be the target of resistance. Occasionally, the state may even be an agent of resistance, e.g. in some measure, Malaysia's application of capital controls and France's measured response to the 'Washington consensus' on deregulation, liberalization, and privatization.

Incorporating certain dimensions of a Gramscian perspective, another frame is James C. Scott's idea of 'infrapolitics': everyday forms of resistance adopted singularly or collectively, but not openly declared contestations (1990). Infrapolitical activities emerge in the context of public transcripts (the self-portraits of dominant elites), and may take various forms, such as gossip, foot-dragging, squatting, and humor. Hidden transcripts are the record of what subordinate groups say and do beyond the realm of the public transcript. They register infrapolitical activities that contest, often very subtly, practices of domination, and may be construed as counterdiscourses. The danger with this broad category, however, is overworking it, i.e. considering every sort of reaction to globalization as resistance and using a wide gamut of forms of resistance as a catch-all without gauging their actual impact on macrostructures.

As distinct from Polanyi, Gramsci, and Scott, Foucault delimits unfamiliar bounds of resistance. For him, power and resistance are mutually constitutive in that every power relationship involves a contest of opposing strategies for structuring power relationships. Yet resistance is not the flip side of power, which, in a Foucaultian sense, is extremely broad, perhaps unduly so; it is everywhere. 'Just as the network of power relations ends by forming a dense web that passes through apparatuses and institutions, without being exactly localized in them, so too the swarm of points of resistance traverse social stratifications and individual unities' (1990: 96). Power tends toward totalizing and hierarchical organizations, but resistance is decentralized, local, and unique. 'Hence there is no single locus of great Refusal. . . . Instead there is a plurality of resistances, each of them a special case. . . .' (1990: 95–6).

In other words, if power is best understood as a flow that forms a vast multiplicity, then resistance itself is multiple – therefore, highly diffuse – and often localized. It is Foucault's insight that resistance may be a flat, non-hierarchical network of power relations and that it creates a local knowledge to counter repressive power, a point that may be used, in conjunction with other frames, to illuminate Southeast Asia's encounters with globalization.

Southeast Asia

To examine resistance to globalization, there is no substitute for a fine-grained analysis of specific world regions and subregions. With its rich, multilayered history and enormous diversity, Southeast Asia offers an excellent vantage point for viewing globalization and myriad responses to it. The 1997–8 Asian economic crisis called attention to the ways in which global flows deeply affect the subregion of Southeast Asia, not least its major cities, which had been regarded as epicenters of 'miracle' and 'near-miracle' economies. To varying degrees of vulnerability, ranging from a heavily affected country such as Indonesia to the more resilient Singapore, the crisis drove the subregion into a downward spiral that was not only economic, but also had political, social, and ecological ramifications.

The 1997–8 crisis may come to be seen as a harbinger of a succession of crises in globalization, a pervasive feature of the twenty-first century. So, too, the responses to it, points on a spectrum (not a binary opposition) from compliance to resistance, suggest an assortment of creative possibilities for remapping globalization. Indeed, insofar as globalization is not a unitary structure, it in no manner homogenizes all social phenomena, but articulates with them in varied ways to produce diverse outcomes. If so, the resistance can strive to build a pluralist, open, and tolerant world order. Insofar as resistance entails a desire to surmount the intolerable, then it is a matter of remembering not an idyllic past but the histories of local attempts to rectify grievances against injustice. In some parts of Southeast Asia, as with the mobilizations in the Philippines against Spanish colonialism, US domination, and military rule, there is a long tradition and living memory of redressing grievances. Although under other conditions, culture, as in Malaysia, may constrain, up to a point, the overt expression of conflict, agents – coalitions of social forces – will, in some cases, nonetheless act against harms inflicted on them (e.g. see Sabihah's study of Sarawak 2001). These forms of collective action have the potential to spill over to an enlarged social space and other political jurisdictions. Yet it is worth emphasizing that resistance is not merely a negation of an existing abuse. Resistance, and alterglobalization writ large, is also a matter of imagining something better than the present order.

The scale of globalization

Imagining the scale of political community is a time-honored tradition in political philosophy. Reflecting on spatial scale in the ideal state, Aristotle held that the territory of the polis should be of moderate size – in a physical *and* intersubjective sense, for he was mindful of identity – and easily surveyable: 'In point of *extent* and size, the territory should be large enough to enable its inhabitants to live a life of leisure which combines liberality with temperance' (Aristotle 1962: 293, italics in original). More recently, given myriad pressures on the territorial state from above and below, globalization is about a quest for an appropriate temporal and spatial scale for social organization. Inasmuch as globalization is not a single, but a complex of interconnected, processes with different vectors in various world regions, it is a multiscalar phenomenon (Jessop 1997, 1999; Mittelman 2000). And, as indicated, the pressures on it join structural forces, such as market dynamics or state-led regionalism, and agential elements, as in the activities of social movements.

It is no coincidence that social movements – the word movement itself denoting changes in locus – strategize in terms of scaling up, out, and down. Scaling up takes place when groups within civil society broaden their impact by building links with other sectors and extending the scope of multisectoral initiatives beyond the local area. This may involve thrusting out of the national state to forge ties with civil societies in other countries or regions. Operationally, however, if globalization's architecture is perceived as too huge for local life, scaling up and out may cause disorientation. The ambiguity rendered by globalization, in some instances, causes a paradoxical response, which is to scale down: to erect a fortress around the community and to localize without engaging the forces of globalization.

In modern times, the main political unit has, of course, been the state, inaugurated in the West and grafted on to other parts of the world. The territorial model of political organization requires that sovereign states attempt to control cross-border flows and affirm the logic of the interstate system. Economic globalization, however, entails an acceleration of transnational flows – capital, technology, information, migration, and the like – that slice across territorial boundaries. The horizontal connections forged in the world economy and the vertical dimensions of state politics are two different vectors of social organization, with the latter seeking to accommodate changing global structures. Whereas the former is large, remote, and lacking accountability, the latter is more proximate to citizens and increasingly subject to pressures for more accountability. In this disjuncture, space is expanding, and new venues are opening, for resistance activities. With globalization, nonstate politics takes on greater salience.

Although it is argued that globalization means deterritorialization – the growth of supraterritorial relations (e.g. Scholte 2000) – much of the resistance, in fact, centers on reterritorialization. Whereas democracy has been framed for territorially bounded states that purportedly can contain the movement of people, ideas, and technologies, efforts are under way to reterritorialize democracy. This means strengthening democracy within and across state borders as a method of governance for solving regional and global problems. Various resistance campaigns are attempting to rebuild political community and social solidarity on a temporal and spatial scale appropriate for a globalizing age. These campaigns largely emanate from civil society, and while some states serve as courtesans for market forces, states may also resist globalizing structures. If so, and more as a matter of potential than as a current pattern, the efforts of civil societies and states can invigorate one another in a mutual attempt to remap globalization.

The question of territorial units and, more generally, of scale is taken further in the debate over whether the knowledge claims embodied in globalization studies form an ascendant paradigm.

3 Globalization: an ascendant paradigm?

This chapter explores the question, does globalization constitute an ascendant paradigm in international studies? Put in perspective, this question goes beyond our field's three 'great debates' over ontology, methodology, and epistemology. Now another debate, which focuses on globalization as a paradigmatic challenge, is heating up, kindling theoretical controversies, and fusing the issues vetted in earlier rounds. The first debate was waged between 'realists' and 'idealists'; the second, 'traditionalists' and 'scientists'; the third, 'positivists' versus 'post-positivists', or 'mainstreamers' versus 'dissidents' (in the terms of Lapid 1989; Wendt 1999: 39; Puchala 2000: 136).

Now, it is time to move on. International studies is on the cusp of a debate between those whom I will call *para-keepers*, observers who are steadfast about maintaining the prevailing paradigms and deny that globalization offers a fresh way of thinking about the world, and *para-makers*, who bring into question what they regard as outmoded categories and claim to have shifted to an innovatory paradigm. This distinction is a heuristic for examining multiple theses. The ensuing heuristic argument does not posit a relation between two positions such that one is the absence of the other. Rather, between the keepers and the makers there are many gradations and dynamic interactions. These are tendencies, not absolutes. Similarly, there is not a binary debate between an extant globalization paradigm and the possibility of an alterglobalization paradigm. As this chapter will show, myriad points and complex interpretations mark the intellectual landscape.

In international studies, ascendancy to a new *paradigm* would indicate something other, or more, than the fourth, a successor, in a sequential progression of debates. True, building new knowledge may be a cumulative process, but it is not necessarily a linear one, and only occasionally involves paradigmatic rupture. To be sure, paradigms do not shift frequently, quickly, or easily. International studies specialists are supposed to be the knowers, but, frankly speaking, often follow the doers in the sense that we trail events, even massive ones, as with our failure to anticipate the end of the Cold War, and still resist changing the paradigms in which many of us are invested.

If a paradigm in Thomas Kuhn's sense (1970) is understood to mean a common framework, a shared worldview that helps to define problems, a set of tools and methods, and modes of resolving the research questions deemed askable, then globalization studies makes for strange bedfellows. Perhaps constituting an up-and-coming subfield within international studies, globalization research brings together different types of theorists, with varied commitments and stakes.

No one would deny that globalization is the subject of a rapidly proliferating theoretical literature. Notwithstanding its antecedents, primarily studies in classical social theory and world history, and on the rise of capitalism, a scholarly literature on globalization per se did not really exist before the 1990s. To a certain extent, globalization is a synthetic concept – a reconstruction of precursor concepts through which analysts seek to comprehend reality. Clearly, this reconstruction is of recent vintage, and the literature and contestation over its importance go to the heart of our field. What is the fundamental problematic in international studies? Primarily peace and war? Mainly what states do to each other? Rather, states and markets, a binary in much teaching and research on international political economy (even though Strange [1996, 1998] and others exploded it to include a wide variety of nonstate actors)? Or, if globalization really strikes a new chord, how does it change the problematic, and what are the implications for the ways in which disciplinary, cross-national, development, and area studies relate to international studies?

In this chapter, then, the objective is to pull together the divergent positions, which heretofore are fragmented and may be found in many scattered sources, on the question of the ascendany of globalization as a knowledge set and the formation of a new paradigm.[1] I want to frame and sharpen the debate, and seek to strike a balance, though not necessarily midway, along a continuum, marked on either end by the resolute arguments put forward by the para-keepers and the more grandiose claims of the para-makers. In so doing, I will stake out postulates in globalization studies, disclose its inadequacies, and note the explanatory potential.

An emerging debate

In the evolving debate, it is worth repeating, there are different shadings on a spectrum, not a sharp dichotomy, between para-keepers and para-makers. Indeed, in time, the para-makers may become wedded to keeping their paradigm and experience attacks by other para-makers. To discern their positions in respect to globalization, one can illustrate – not provide comprehensive coverage – by invoking explicit statements expressing the commitments of scholars and by examining logical extensions of their arguments, while taking care, of course, not to do injustice to them.

The keepers are naysayers who doubt or deny that globalization constitutes an ascendant paradigm. They include realists, interdependence theorists, social democrats, and some world-system theorists. Regarding globalization as 'the fad of the 1990s' and as a model lacking evidence, Kenneth Waltz declares that contrary to the claims of theorists whom he calls 'globalizers' – what I take to be a shorthand for globalization researchers – 'politics, as usual, prevails over economics' (1999: 694, 696, 700). Reaffirming the neorealist position that 'national interests' continue to drive the 'interstate system' – advanced two decades earlier (Waltz 1979) – he does not examine the foundational theoretical literature written by 'globalizers' who worry about the same problems that concern him. Surprisingly, Waltz fails to identify major pioneering theoreticians (such as Giddens 1990; Harvey 1990; and Robertson 1992), opposing points of view, and different schools of globalization studies. Waltz would probably find much to respect and much to correct in this work. Recalling Robert Keohane and Joseph Nye's 1977 book, *Power and Interdependence*, Waltz's point (1999) is that the globalizers' contention about interdependence reaching a new level is not unlike the earlier claim that simple interdependence had become complex interdependence, i.e. countries are increasingly connected by varied social and political relationships and to a lesser degree by matters of security and force.

In fact, more recently, Keohane and Nye maintained that contemporary globalization is not entirely new: 'Our characterization of interdependence more than 20 years ago now applies to globalization at the turn of the millennium' (2000: 104). Thus, like complex interdependence, the concept of globalization can be fruitfully extended to take into account networks that operate at 'multi-continental distances', the greater density of these networks, and the increased number of actors participating in them (Keohane and Nye 2000). In comparison to Waltz, Keohane and Nye reach beyond classic themes in politics to allow for more changes, and build transnational issues into their framework. However, like Waltz, Keohane and Nye (1998) posit that the system of state sovereignty is resilient and remains the dominant structure in the world. Implicit in their formulation is that the state-centered paradigm is the best-suited approach to globalization; by inference, it can be adjusted so long as it is utilized in an additive manner, i.e. incorporates more dimensions into the analysis.

Not only do interdependence theorists (and neoliberal institutionalists, in Keohane's sense of the term, 1984) seek to assimilate globalization to tried and tested approaches in international studies, but also social democrats have similarly argued that there is nothing really new about globalization. By extension, from this standpoint, a new theoretical departure is unwarranted. In an influential study, Paul Hirst and Grahame Thompson (1999, echoing Gordon 1988) claim that the world economy is not really global, but centered on the triad of Europe, Japan, and North America, as empirically demonstrated by flows of trade, foreign direct investment, and finance. They argue that the current level of internationalized activities is not unprecedented; the world economy is not as open and integrated as it was in the period from 1870 to 1914; and today, the major powers continue to harmonize policy, as they did before. Leaving aside methodological questions about the adequacy of their empirical measures and the matter of alternative indicators (see Mittelman 2000: 9–24), clearly Hirst and Thompson adhere to a Weberian mode of analysis consisting of a dichotomy between two ideal types, an inter-national economy based on exchange between separate national economies versus a full-fledged global economy. Taking issue with advocates of free markets who, the authors believe, exaggerate globalizing tendencies and want to diminish regulation, Hirst and Thompson, on the contrary, favor more extensive political control of markets – greater regulation.

World-system theorists also contend that there is nothing new about globalization, a phenomenon that can be traced back many centuries to the origins of capitalism (Wallerstein 2000) or even earlier. From this perspective, it is argued that the basic conflict is between a capitalist world-system and a socialist world-system. However, as will be discussed, the point of much globalization research is to expand binaries, such as the inter-national versus the global and capitalism versus socialism, so as to allow for multiple *globalizing* processes, including at the macroregional, subregional, and microregional levels as well as in localities. If anything, globalization blurs many dualities – state and nonstate, legal and illegal, public and private, and so on – that are customary in international studies.

Coming down differently on the debate over globalization *qua* paradigm are diverse theorists who resist pigeonholing into any particular tradition or traditions, yet all of whom support the proposition that globalization constitutes a distinctive theoretical innovation. However difficult to categorize collectively, this transatlantic group of authors signals the stirrings of a paradigmatic challenge to international studies. Emblematic of this position are the writings of four scholars with different commitments but whose position on new knowledge converges.

Representative of the innovatory stance is Philip Cerny's assertion that theorists are seeking an alternative to realism and that 'the chief contender for that honour has been the concept of globalization' (1996: 618). Similarly, Ian Clark's *Globalization and International Relations Theory* makes the unequivocal argument that 'globalization offers a framework within which political change can be understood' and that 'if globalization does anything, it makes possible a theory of change' (1999: 174). Joining Cerny and Clark, Jan Aart Scholte holds that '[c]ontemporary globalisation gives ample cause for a paradigm shift' (1999: 9), or, in another formulation, 'the case that globalism warrants a paradigm shift would seem to be incontrovertible' (1999: 22). Although Scholte does fill in some of the blanks, the question still is, what are the characteristics of this new paradigm?

While globalization theorists have tentatively, but not systematically, responded to this question (an issue to which I will return), there is also a more guarded intervention in the debate over globalization's status as a paradigm. Noting 'parametric transformations' in world order, James Rosenau (1997) clearly sides with those who affirm that globalization forms a new point of paradigmatic departure. However, he holds that his concept of globalization is 'narrower in scope and more specific in content' than are many other concepts associated with changing global structures. According to Rosenau, globalization refers to 'processes, to sequences that unfold either *in the mind* or in behavior' as people and organizations attempt to achieve their goals (1997: 80; emphasis added). In other words, globalization is not only an objective trend, but also constitutes, or is constituted by, subjective processes. It is a mental, or intersubjective, framework that is implicated both in the exercise of power and in scholarship that informs, or is critical of, public policy. Certainly, because of the need for greater theoretical, as well as empirical, precision, a qualified response to the question of the rise of a new paradigm is worthy of consideration. The route to this response will be a Kuhnian notion of what sparks paradigmatic transformations.

The question of new knowledge[2]

In his study of the history of the natural sciences, Kuhn (1970) famously argued that new paradigms appear through ruptures rather than through a linear accumulation of facts or hypotheses. Normal science, he claimed, is a means of confirming the type of knowledge already established and legitimized by the paradigm in which it arises. According to Kuhn, normal science often suppresses innovations because they are subversive of a discipline's fundamental commitments:

> No part of the aim of normal science is to call forth new sorts of phenomena; indeed those that will not fit the box are often not seen at all. Nor do scientists normally aim to invent new theories, and they are often intolerant of those invented by others. Instead, normal-scientific research is directed to the articulation of those phenomena and theories that the paradigm already supplies.
>
> (Kuhn 1970: 24)

Or, to extrapolate, one might say that members of a shared knowledge community not only normalize certain types of questions, but also suppress the ability to raise other kinds of questions. Most important, Kuhn's insight is that only rarely do intellectuals refuse to accept the evasion of anomalies: observations at odds with expectations derived from prior theoretical understandings. A new paradigm emerges when the burden of anomalous phenomena grows too great and when there is incommensurability between competing paradigms to the extent that proponents of alternative frameworks cannot accept a common ground of assumptions.

Some observers dispute whether Kuhn's thesis, derived from the natural sciences, can be imported into the social sciences – and, I might add, into a field like international studies, which is far more heterogeneous than disciplines such as physics. My concern here, however, is not the epistemological debate over the disparate means of discovery in respective branches of knowledge (see Lakatos 1970; Ball 1976; Barnes 1982). Rather, my contention – that globalization is not only about 'real' phenomena, but also a way of interpreting the world – is more pragmatic.

To be sure, a Kuhnian perspective on the generation of knowledge is vulnerable insofar as it is limited to social and psychological conditions within the scientific community, and does not give sufficient credence to socially constructed knowledge outside this community. The factors internal to the social sciences cannot be fully explained without reference to the external elements. There is nothing, however, to prevent joining Kuhn's insight about theoretical innovation with a broader analysis of social conditions. Moreover, unless one believes that international studies is rapidly approaching a Kuhnian crisis, i.e. the overthrow of a reigning paradigm or paradigms – and I do not – then it is important to grasp the dynamic interface between established knowledge sets, including the structures (curricula, professional journals, funding agencies, etc.) that maintain and undermine them, and a potentially new paradigm. It would appear that even without a paradigm crisis, an ascendant paradigm could emerge.

For Kuhn, the transition to a new paradigm is all or nothing: 'Like the gestalt switch, it must occur all at once (though not necessarily in an instant) or not at all' (Kuhn 1970: 150; also pertinent are the nuances in his subsequent work, 1977a, 1977b). In explaining transformations in this manner, Kuhn falls short insofar as he underestimates the tenacity of forerunner paradigms and their ability to modify themselves. By all indications in the social sciences, they fight back, usually with gusto. Nevertheless, by identifying the propellant of a new paradigm as the refusal to accept the evasion of anomalies in conjunction with the quest for an alternative, Kuhn has contributed powerfully to understanding theoretical innovation.

In this vein, it is well to recall Weber's '"Objectivity" in Social Science and Social Policy' (1949). Like Kuhn, Weber indicated that the prevailing intellectual apparatus is in constant tension with new knowledge. According to Weber, this conflict is a propellant for creativity and discovery: concepts are and should be subject to change. However, there should also be a certain staying power in the intellectual apparatus that enables one to ferret out what is worth knowing. In other words, there is nothing worse than the fads and fashions that come in and go out of vogue. In the end, Weber called for a mid-course between unyielding old concepts and unceasing shifts in paradigms.

Following Kuhn and Weber in the chase for paradigmatic advance, what are the anomalies in our field, and is globalization a viable contender for fixing these imperfections?

Discomfort with international studies

A discipline without complaints would be a *non-sequitur*. After all, scholars are trained in the art of debate; the skills of nuance are our stock-in-trade. That said, it is important to consider the specific anomalies within international studies. Although some of these anomalies are perennial, it is no wonder that others have recently appeared, given monumental changes after the Cold War, and with the distinctive mix of global integration and disintegration at the dawn of a new millennium. While others could be cited, five anomalies seem most important, but can be considered only succinctly here.

First, the term *international* studies suggests a focus on relations between nations. But this is not so. The discipline has primarily concerned relations between states, the nation being only one of many principles of social organization (Shaw 1994: 25; also see Shaw 1999). Closely related, observers (e.g. Rosenau 1997; Baker 2000: 366) have long argued that the conventional distinction between separate national and international spheres of activity is misleading. Nowadays, it is increasingly difficult to maintain the lines of demarcation between the domestic and the foreign realms, or between comparative politics and international politics. Globalization means that the distinction between them is hard to enforce. Increasingly evident are myriad forms of interpenetration between the global and the national – global economic actors even exist within the state, as with global crime groups in Russia or the IMF/World Bank's structural adjustment programs in developing countries.

Thus, a third discontent is opposition to the persistence of state centrism. From this angle, the case for an ontological shift springs from the anomaly between the objects of study seen through a realist or neorealist lens and globalists' vision of a polycentric, or multilevel, world order. New ontological priorities – an issue to which I will return – would consist of a series of linked processes. Toward this end, globalization researchers are attempting to design a framework for interrelating economics, politics, culture, and society in a seamless web. Hence, in large measure as a response to globalization, some scholars have shifted their attention to global governance in an effort to incorporate a broader ontology of structures and agents. The state is treated as one among several actors. It is not that state sovereignty is losing meaning, but that the multilevel environment in which it operates, and hence the meaning of the concept, is changing.

Methodologically, the field of *international* studies is based on the premise of territoriality, reflected in central concepts such as state-centered nationalism, state borders, and state sovereignty. Yet, with the development of new technologies, especially in communications and transportation, the advent of a 'network society' (Castells 1996), and the emergence of a 'nonterritorial region' (Ruggie 1993), there is a marked shift toward a more deterritorialized world. Hence, Scholte has challenged 'methodological territorialism' – the ingrained practice of formulating questions, gathering data, and arriving at conclusions all through the prism of a territorial framework (1999: 17; and 2000). Without swinging to the opposite extreme of adopting a 'globalist methodology' by totally rejecting the importance of the principle of territoriality, Scholte calls for a 'full-scale methodological reorientation', and concludes '[T]hat globalisation warrants a paradigm shift would seem to be incontrovertible' (1999: 21–2).

Finally, there is the postmodernist complaint, which, arguably, has not really registered in our field.[3] As Edward Said (1979) contends in regard to Orientalism, it is hard to erase certain representations of reality, for in Foucaultian terms, they take on the aura of authoritative expressions and are implicated in the exercise of power. Knowledge sets may thus operate as closed systems – what Steven Caton (1999: 8) terms 'endless cycles of self-referring statements' – thwarting counter-representations that might have the power to challenge normal knowledge. As scholars in international studies, perhaps we should reflect on this allegation about collectively self-referential work, for we spend an enormous amount of time engaging in intramural debates over concepts, often without paying sufficient attention to the phenomena themselves. Still, it would be wrong to gloss over Said's insight that representations made manifest as knowledge are tied to the establishment, maintenance, and exercise of power. In international studies, probing Said's point about reflexivity involves shifting explanatory levels above and below the state – a characteristic of globalization research.

Characteristics of globalization studies

Globalization theorists, of course, are not univocal. Inasmuch as their writings abound, there are different interpretations and considerable contestation. As Donald Puchala aptly put it, '[C]onventional theories all have a table of outcomes that inventory what needs to be explained (2001)'. For example, the realist table of outcomes is chiefly wars, alliances, balances of power, and arms races. For liberals, the outcomes are regimes, integration, cooperation, and hegemons (Puchala 2001). By contrast, the problematic that globalization theorists seek to explain, while dynamic and open-ended, not invariant, may be gleaned from an emerging series of core, linked propositions. I will highlight six of them.

1   Many contemporary problems cannot be explained as interactions among nation states, i.e. as international studies, but must be construed as global problems. Although this claim is not unique to globalization studies, at issue is a series of problems, e.g. the rise of organized crime, global warming, and the spread of infectious diseases – partly within and partly across borders, partially addressed by states and partially beyond their regulatory framework.

2   Globalization constitutes a structural transformation in world order. As such, it is about not only the here-and-now, but also warrants a long perspective of time and revives the study of space. A preoccupation with what Fernand Braudel (1980: 3, 27), and François Simiand before him, called 'the history of events' – the immediate moment – focuses attention on a frame that differs from the *longue durée*, an observation point that some researchers find advantageous for viewing the spatial reorganization of the global economy (a theme to which we will return in Chapter 4 on 'Critical Globalization Studies').

3   As a transformation, globalization involves a series of continuities and discontinuities with the past. In other words, the globalization tendency is by no means a total break – as noted, there is considerable disagreement about how much is new – but the contemporary period is punctuated by large-scale acceleration in globalizing processes, such as the integration of financial markets, technological development, and intercultural contact.

4   New ontological priorities are warranted because of the emergence of a dialectic of suprastate and substate forces, pressures from above and from below. The advent of an ontology of globalization is fluid, by no means fixed. It includes the global economy as an actor in its own right (as embodied, for example, in transnational corporations), states and interstate organizations, regionalist processes (at the macro, sub, and micro-levels), world cities, and civil society, sometimes manifest as social movements.

5   Given shifting parameters, the state, in turn, seeks to adjust to evolving global structures. States, however, are in varied positions vis-à-vis globalizing forces,

and re-invent themselves differently, the gamut of policies running from a full embrace, as with New Zealand's extreme neoliberal policies from 1984 to 1999, to resistance, illustrated by Malaysia's capital controls in 1998.

6   Underpinning such differences is a set of new, or deeper, tensions in world order, especially the disjuncture between the principle of territoriality, fundamental to the concept of state sovereignty, and the patent trend toward deterritorialization, especially, but not only, apparent in regard to transborder economic flows. The horizontal connections forged in the world economy and the vertical dimensions of state politics are two dissimilar vectors of social organization, with the latter seeking to accommodate the changing global matrix.

However schematically presented, the aforementioned, interrelated propositions put into question some of international studies' ingrained ways of conceptualizing the world. At present, although the attempts at reconceptualization are in a preliminary stage of formulation, it is worth identifying the traps and confusions.

Discomfort with paradigmatic pretension

Barring caricatures of the concept *and* phenomena of globalization, e.g. it is totalizing, inevitable, and homogenizing, rather than, as many scholars maintain, partial, open-ended, and hybrid, surely there are grounds for discontent. For one thing, globalization may be seen as a slippery concept. Hence, the complaint lodged earlier in this chapter: observers (e.g. A. T. Kearney, Inc. 2003) are crying out and striving for more analytical precision.

Moreover, globalization is sometimes deemed overdetermined – too abstract, too structural, and insufficiently attentive to agency. From this perspective, it is thought that the logic is mechanically specified or misspecified in that it is too reductive. For some, especially scholars carrying out contextualized, fine-grained research on particular issues and distinct areas, globalization is regarded as too blunt a tool. After all, what does it leave out? What is not globalization? In response, it may be argued that globalization is mediated by other processes and actors, including the state. Furthermore, globalization has a direct or indirect impact on various levels of social organization, and becomes inserted into the local, thus complicating the distinction between the global and the local.

Another problem, then, is that the globalization literature has spawned its own binary oppositions. On the one hand, as indicated, the phenomena of globalization blur dichotomous distinctions to which international studies has grown accustomed. For example, civil society now penetrates the state (as with members of environmental movements assuming important portfolios in government in the Philippines; and in several African countries, state substitution is abundantly evident – some so-called 'nongovernmental organizations' (NGOs) are sustained by state funding or, arguably, their agendas are driven by the state or interstate organizations). On the other hand, globalization research itself presents new binary choices – 'globalization from above' and 'globalization from below', top–down and bottom–up globalization, and so on – that certainly have heuristic value but must be exploded in order to capture the range of empirical phenomena.

How far have we come?

It would be remiss not to join a discussion of the drawbacks to globalization as an avenue of inquiry with its real gains, even if the nature of a new paradigm is tentative and contested.

In the main, globalization studies emphasizes the historicity of all social phenomena. There is no escaping historiography. What are the driving forces behind globalization, and when did it originate? With the beginnings of inter-cultural contact, the dawn of capitalism in Western Europe in the long sixteenth century, or in a distinct conjuncture after World War II? Research has thus opened new questions for investigation and debate. And even if one returns to old issues, such as theories of the state, there are opposing views and vexing questions, especially in the face of public representations, such as Margaret Thatcher's attack on the 'nanny state'. Per the discussion above (Chapter 1), should the state be construed as in retreat (Strange 1996), as an agent of globalization (Cox, R.W. 1987), or, in an even more activist role, as the driver of globalization (Panitch 1996; or from another perspective, Weiss 1998)? Taken together, the writings on these issues combat the fragmentation of knowledge. Not surprisingly, given the themes that globalization embraces – technology, ecology, films, health, fast-food and other consumer goods, and so on – it is transdisciplinary, involving not exclusively the social sciences, but also the natural sciences, the humanities, and professional fields such as architecture, law, and medicine.

Arguably, within the social sciences, economic and political geographers (including Dicken 2003; Harvey 1999; Knox and Agnew 1998; Olds 2001; Taylor 1993; Taylor, Johnson, and Watts 1995; Thrift 1996) have carried out some of the most sophisticated research on globalization. Even though the importance of spatial concerns is increasingly apparent, many international studies specialists have not noticed the work of economic and political geographers.

For the purposes of teaching globalization, one way to draw students into a subject that, after all, involves thinking about big, abstract structures, is to focus on spatial issues as they relate to the changes in one's own locale. Reading a collection of essays consisting of anthropological fieldwork at McDonald's restaurants in different Asian countries (Watson 1997), and then comparing the findings in the literature to their own fieldwork, including interviewing employees and customers at a nearby McDonald's, my students are asked to analyze the cultural political economy of globalization: a production system, the composition of the labor force (largely immigrants and members of minority groups in our locale), social technologies, and the representations conveyed by symbols. The students pursue the question of meanings – the intersubjective dimensions of globalization – in the writings of not only social scientists (Ritzer 2000) but architects, e.g. on shopping malls and theme parks (Sorkin 1992), and by visits to local sites.

Time permitting, consideration is also given to the legal and medical spheres. Cybergangs and some novel types of crime do not neatly fit into the jurisdiction of national or international law (see, for example, Sassen 1998). The field of public health has called attention to the nexus of social *and* medical problems, especially with the spread of AIDS. The tangible consequences of a changing global division of labor and power include new flows and directions of migration, the separation of families, a generation of orphans, and the introduction of the HIV virus into rural areas by returning emigrants. As these topics suggest, globalization studies identifies silences and establishes new intellectual space – certainly one criterion by which to gauge an ascendant paradigm.

Pushing the agenda

Notwithstanding important innovations, as a paradigm, globalization is more of a potential than a refined framework, worldview, kit of tools and methods, and mode of resolving questions. Where, then, do we go from here? Although these are not the only issues, the following challenges stand out as central to developing globalization studies:

1   Just as with capitalism, which has identifiable variants, there is no single, unified form of globalization. Researchers have not yet really mapped the different forms of globalization, which in the literature is sometimes preceded by adjectival designations such as 'neoliberal', 'disembedded', 'centralizing', 'Islamic', 'inner and outer', or 'democratic'. The adjectival labels are but hints at the need for systematic study of the varieties. Or should the object of study be *globalizations*?[4]

2   Closely related is the problem of how to depict the genres of globalization research. What are the leading schools of thought? How to classify them so as to organize this massive literature and advance investigation? To catalog globalization studies according to national traditions of scholarship, by disciplinary perspective, or on single issues risks mistaking the parts for the whole. Avoiding this trap, Mauro Guillén (2001) decongests the burgeoning globalization research by organizing it into key debates. Is globalization really happening, does it produce convergence, does it undermine the authority of nation-states, is globality different from modernity, and is a global culture in the making? In another stocktaking, David Held *et al.* (1999) sort the field into hyperglobalizers, who believe that the growth of world markets diminishes the role of states; skeptics, who maintain that international interactions are not novel and that states have the power to regulate international economic flows; and transformationalists, who claim that new patterns and an unprecedented configuration of global power relations have emerged. But there are other debates, major differences among policy research (Rodrik 1997), structural approaches (Falk 1999), and critical/poststructural accounts (Hardt and Negri 2000).

3   What are the implications of globalization for disciplinary and cross-national studies? How should these domains of knowledge respond to the globalization

challenge? It would seem that in light of the distinctive combinations of evolving global structures and local conditions in various regions, globalization enhances, not reduces, the importance of the comparative method. However, there is the matter of exploring disciplinary and comparative themes within changing parameters and examining the interactions between these parameters and the localities.

4   Similarly, what does globalization mean for development and area studies? Philip McMichael (2004: 152) holds that '[t]he globalization project succeeded the development project'. Surely development theory emerged in response to a particular historical moment: the inception of the Cold War, which, if anything, was an ordering principle in world affairs. After the sudden demise of this structure, development studies reached a conceptual cul-de-sac. Put more delicately, it may be worth revisiting development studies' basic tenets, especially apropos the dynamics of economic growth and the mechanisms of political power in the poorest countries, which have experienced a fundamental erosion of the extent of control that they had maintained – however little to begin with. This loss has been accompanied by changing priorities and reorganizations within funding agencies, a crucial consideration in terms of support for training the next generation of scholars, particularly apparent with regard to fieldwork for dissertations. Although some para-keeper area specialists have dug in their heels and have fought to protect normal knowledge in their domain, the task is to re-invent and thereby strengthen area studies.

5   Insufficient scholarly attention has centered on the ethics of globalization. The telling question is, what and whose values are inscribed in globalization? In light of the unevenness of globalization, with large zones of marginalization (not only in a spatial sense, but also in terms of race, ethnicity, gender, and who is or is not networked), there is another searching question, is globalization ethically sustainable? What is the relationship between spirituality and globalization, an issue posed by different religious movements? Which contemporary Weberian will step forward to write *The Neoliberal Ethic and the Spirit of Globalization?*

6   Emanating mostly from the West, globalization studies is not really global. In terms of participating researchers and the focus of inquiry, there is a need for decentering. The literature on globalization unavailable in the English language (e.g. Ferrer 1997; Gómez 2000; Kaneko 1999; Norani and Mandal 2000; Podestà *et al.* 2000) is rarely taken into account in the English-speaking world. Still, only limited work has thus far emerged in the developing world, including studies undertaken by the Council for the Development of Economic and Social Research in Africa (1998, 2002), the National University of Singapore (Olds *et al.* 1999), the Latin American Social Sciences Council (Seoane and Taddei 2001), and the Institute of Malaysian and International Studies at the National University of Malaysia (Mittelman and Norani 2001).

7   Apart from the development of individual courses, there is a lack of systematic thought about the programmatic implications of globalization for the

academy. Does global restructuring warrant academic restructuring in the ways in which knowledge is organized for students? If a new paradigm is emerging, what does this mean in terms of pedagogy and curriculum?[5] Will universities, and their international studies specialists, be in the forefront of or trail behind changes in world order? Will they really open to the innovation of globalization studies?

To sum up, it is worth recalling that on more than one occasion Susan Strange held that international studies is like an open range, home to many different types of research. Today, there is diversity, but surely one should not overlook the fences that hold back the strays. Mavericks who work in non-Western discourses, economic and political geographers, postmodernists and poststructuralists, not to mention humanists (whose contributions are emphasized by Alker 1996; Puchala 2000; and others), have faced real barriers.

It is in this context that globalization studies has emerged as a means to explain the intricacy and variability of the ways in which the world is restructuring and, by extension, to assess reflexively the categories used by social scientists to analyze these phenomena. The para-keepers, to varying degrees, are reluctant to embrace globalization as a knowledge set because some of its core propositions challenge predominant ontological, methodological, and epistemological commitments – what Kuhn referred to as 'normal science'. Again, not to dichotomize positions but to look to the other end of the spectrum, para-makers advance a strong thesis about the extent to which a new paradigm is gaining ascendancy. The debate is fruitful in that it engages in theoretical stocktaking, locates important problem areas, and points to possible avenues of inquiry. It also helps to delimit space for investigation and to identify venues of intellectual activity. But, in the near term, there is no looming Kuhnian crisis in the sense of an impending overthrow that would quickly sweep away reigning paradigms. Given that systematic research on globalization is only slightly more than a decade in the making, it is more likely that international studies has entered an interregnum between the old and the new.

Although globalization studies entails a putting together of bold efforts to theorize structural change, it would be wrong either to underestimate or to exaggerate the achievements. Judging the arguments in the debate, on balance, a modest thesis is in order. The efforts to theorize globalization have produced a patchwork, an intellectual move rather than a movement, and more of a potential than worked-out alternatives to accepted ways of thinking in international studies. In sum, this fledgling may be regarded as a proto-paradigm.

At this stage, there are different paradigmatic tendencies. It would be reductionist to suggest that the knowledge set under the umbrella of alter-globalization can be neatly distinguished from other sets. Although there is not a bifurcation between globalization studies and alterglobalization studies, the knowledge that comprises alterglobalization is rooted in critical theory and its core is readily identifiable.

4   Critical globalization studies

In the burgeoning of globalization studies, different kinds of knowledge overlap and are variously described as historical, empirical, formal, intuitive, theoretical, and critical knowledge sets.[1] The levels of abstraction range from basic to applied, with room for both theoretical and fire-brigade research. At all levels, there is no dichotomous split between theory and praxis. Both professional and lay theorists, intellectuals who prefer the contemplative life and scholar-activists alike, have contributed importantly to globalization studies.

In the genre of knowledge under consideration here – *critical* globalization studies – scholars are not wedded to any single worldview. There is no universal agreement on how the critical conception should be understood or what characterizes it.

Not surprisingly, critical thinkers' different backgrounds and interests have produced varied emphases. These are linkages between globalization and specific themes, such as cities (Sassen 2001), class structures (Overbeek 2001; Abdul Rahman Embong 2002; Sklair 2002), culture (Robertson 1992; Friedman, J. 1994; Tomlinson 1999; Nederveen Pieterse 2004), development (McMichael 2004; Benería, 2003), the environment (Wapner 2002), ethical life and religion (Held 1995; Falk 1999), gender (Tickner 2001; Peterson 2003), governance (Rosenau 1997; Hettne and Odén 2002), hegemony (Arrighi and Silver 1999; Hardt and Negri 2000), human rights (Cheru 2002), ideology (Rupert 2000; Steger 2002), markets (Dicken 2003; Peck and Yeung 2003), regions (Olds *et al.* 1999; Zeleza 2003), regionalism (Hettne 2002b; Väyrynen 2003) resistance (Gills 2000; Broad 2002; Smith and Johnson 2002; Amoore forthcoming)), the state (Panitch 1996; Robinson 2001), and war and peace (Kaldor 1999). In addition, critical globalization studies offers engaging and insightful textbooks (Scholte 2000; Steger 2003a) and samplers of readings (Robertson and White 2003; Held and McGrew 2003). Public intellectuals outside academe have also produced major statements, partly based on participant-observation, which are integral to critical globalization studies (Barlow and Clarke 2001; Bello 2002; Bové and Dufour 2000; Danaher 2001; Klein 2002; Wallach and Sforza 2000).[2]

Without detailing individual authors' work or tracing the tributaries of critical globalization theory, it is worth identifying the broad commonalities among them. Most important, from a critical perspective, precisely what kind of knowledge about globalization is and should be summoned? What do critical globalization scholars really want to find out? What is the desired knowledge? This chapter is an attempt to answer these guiding questions, at least in a preliminary way.

A critical perspective

On the critical flank, scholars persistently question the positivist faith in empiricism – the distinction between facts and values, the separability of variables, and hypothesis-testing as a means to discover objective 'truth' – and, rather, examine how facts are constructed and whose interests they serve. In the tug of war with positivist knowledge, critical conceptions do not necessarily mean opposition; some scholars and activists, especially the ones mindful of postmodern sensibilities, strive for a multiplicity of conditions that makes room for numerous dominant *and* subaltern positions. A critical perspective can have elements of both conventional and heterodox fields, but does not confuse them and is aware of how they are formed.

At minimum, a critical approach is suspicious, troubling, and open-ended in its search for knowledge. It seeks to reconstruct what Gramsci (1971) called 'common-sense' propositions, which are the product of historical processes that leave the individual in a particular relationship with social groups. For Gramsci, common-sense meanings are multiple, changing, and fragmented among strata. These chaotic conceptions absorb the sediment of folklore, contradict one another, and may not form an entirely coherent whole. Some elements of common sense are consistent with hegemonic stability, while others run counter to it. Critical intellectuals attempt to sharpen the tensions, gain leverage from them, and go against meanings established by institutions such as the mass media, incorporated in cultural goods, and apparent in imaginary realms (e.g. films, television, and magazines). These products can diminish the capacity to think independently and make individuals more susceptible to the language of competitive, globalizing market relations. For Gramsci, critical thinking should not merely oppose but become part of people's understanding of their own conditions, bringing about a new common sense.

To delimit meaningful knowledge, critical scholarship therefore looks to do more than just unmask normal knowledge. A critical orientation calls for not only deconstructing extant knowledge and practice but also constructing new knowledge about what exists and what ought to exist on the basis of transformed relations of power.

Preconceptions

In this vein, international studies may be construed as an impediment to understanding the discourses of globalization. As noted earlier, the main actors are not only states or nations; emergent interactions, tragically exemplified on 9/11, are now occuring between the state-centric and multi-centric worlds (Ferguson and Rosenau 2003).

There is not, however, a bifurcation of two worlds. The state-centric system, like the multi-centric form of world order, harbors diverse forms of state, nonstate modes of governance, and different sources of social solidarity. Just as the state-centric world actively exists within the multi-centric world, so does the multi-centric world operate in the interstices of the state-centric world. To the extent that there is not a complete cleavage between these worlds, one might speak of a *polymorphous* world – orders with many forms that pass through one another. Surely common-sense knowledge does not sufficiently grasp the interpenetration of myriad worlds, perhaps because of the complexity, and, postmodernists would add, the impossibility of delineating a master pattern. As we have seen, globalization complicates categories of analysis and outruns traditional explanations that fail to capture the interplay of market dynamics, power relations, and social forces that slice across borders.

In the reconstruction of knowledge, it is useful to invoke 'standpoint epistemology'. The main theses here are that knowledge must be situated in the material lives of actors; and, in arriving at a standpoint, actors' social locations are crucial. For as Weber had emphasized, a perspective is never total but always partial (Weber 1949, 1971; Harding 1991; Hekman 1997). Before contemporary feminists elaborated this theme about the need for divergent standpoints in knowledge seeking, Braudel (1990) grappled with the importance of viewing phenomena from multiple observation points: different stations in social hierarchies, diverse axes in ordering human affairs, various zones in the global political economy, and distinct speeds of time. In his own research, including a prescient book on civilizations, prepared for the secondary-school syllabus in France but rejected by the intellectual establishment there, Braudel preferred the *longue durée* – the long view of origins and gradual, slow-moving transformations (Chapter 3). Although the long perspective requires patience, it is in no way incompatible with other time frames: what Braudel called the span of the conjuncture (10, 20, or even 50 years) or the immediate period of events (Braudel 1980, 1994). Putting together standpoint epistemology and Braudelian interactions, then, the task is to comprehend multiple orientations within multiple time frames.

Cognizant of the dimensions of hierarchical power relations, time, and space, intellectuals embarked on reconstructing knowledge face the difficult challenge of constructing grounded utopias. I use the term 'grounded utopia' to mean an imagined alternative that has never existed; yet it is a future, or futures, rooted in real historical tendencies and embodied practices. In Weber's sense, the challenge is to achieve 'an ethical *imperative* . . . of what ought to exist' (1949: 91–2; emphasis in original). Without adopting a positivist separation of 'is' and 'ought', globalization critics can usefully work toward a grounded utopia by reconciling Gramsci and Weber such that common sense is reconstituted, its historical contradictions and potentials drawn out, in an attempt to enact the ethics of a desired order.

For his part, Gramsci disavowed a value-free, ahistorical knowledge, exemplified in the pernicious tendencies of both scientism and utopian Marxism. Similarly, while emphasizing that ideal types are methodological constructs, not goals to be realized, Weber cautioned against utopianism in that it underestimates the coercive components of authority and hierarchical social relations, e.g. efforts to eliminate increasingly bureaucratic organizations in the functioning of capitalism (1971: 229). For both Gramsci and Weber, history is powered by structural forces, yet open-ended and free to continuously evolve a new order, not imprisoned by a foreordained or closed schema. So, too, Gramsci and Weber, albeit somewhat differently, emphasized the role of authority and hierarchical institutions in the elevation toward utopias.

Mindful of this intellectual legacy, other theorists pushed the notion of utopia. Just as Polanyi (1957) criticized the 'stark utopia' of a self-regulating market for being ahistorical and then projected a preferred scenario of re-embedding the market in society as a means to increasing freedom, E.H. Carr (1964; with commentary by Cox, M. 2000 and Hettne 2002a), often regarded as the father of realism, held that utopian thinking can cloak interests. Yet he ultimately came down in favor of a balance between an appreciation of power relations and utopian approaches to peace:

> We can describe as utopian in the right sense (i.e. performing the proper function of a utopia in proclaiming an ideal to be aimed at, though not totally attainable) the desire to eliminate the element of power and to base the bargaining process of peaceful change on a common feeling of what is just and reasonable.
>
> (Carr 1964: 222)

In other words, peaceful change requires both utopian visions and critical realist analysis. A common basis among the often divergent perspectives of these thinkers is that grounded utopias can be a valuable heuristic if anchored in history, alert to interests of material power, and attuned to possible means to achieve social justice.

For these theorists, there are hidden aspects of life that lie beneath the visible problems that one encounters. Why? Perhaps power agents want them concealed. For example, when a ruling coalition goes to war, it may reveal some reasons, but others remain undisclosed. Also, certain issues may be uncomfortable to talk about, e.g. self-interest, genocide, ethnic animosity, gendered power structures, and disappearances. To be sure, some contemporary conflicts, as in South Asia, are partly about historical memory, which involves matters of cultural dignity, while others, perhaps such as those in the Middle East today, are in part about humiliation. It may be difficult to forthrightly express these experiences, though in some cases, they have come out in truth commissions.

Even if one would not expect classical theorists to have programmatic answers for the problems of contemporary globalization, it was their insight that something was terribly wrong: for Marx, alienation; for Weber, the iron cage of bureaucratic rationality; and for Durkheim, anomie. Their critical thinking – precursor theories for knowing today's vexed world – emerged in the context of turmoil in Europe: from Marx's perspective, the revolutions of 1848; from Weber's, the social conflicts accompanying Germany's shift from the age of Bismarck to an industrial era; and from Durkheim's, the bouleversements of France's transition from the Third Republic and long revolution to a modern social order. These reflections brought to light the dark side of historical transformations, including the havoc visited on ordinary people (Lemert 1993: 9, 15). The master critical theorists of the nineteenth and early twentieth centuries were suspicious of the common-sense propositions of their day and deeply skeptical about received wisdom. Furthermore, they imagined alternative orders that would alleviate the basic problems of their times.

Traps and confusions

The dawn of the twenty-first century is also a period racked by social turmoil – the disruptions caused by globalizing capitalism, new wars, and a renewed search for meaning in life. What is more, the means of producing knowledge have changed. Today, knowledge is not primarily the work of lone thinkers, but conditioned by powerful material infrastructures – traveling paradigms, funding agencies, think tanks, publishers and journals, professional associations, technologies and networks, and vast research parks. In addition, there are mechanisms for policing knowledge production, such as intellectual property rights, as well as efforts to subvert discursive power.

One way in which these mechanisms operate is through narrative entrapment. There is a danger of entrapping ourselves in worlds of our own making. These worlds can be constructed as language, mental pictures that represent social phenomena, and paradigms that filter ideas inside and keep others outside a knowledge structure (Shotter 1993: 26–31). The risk of falling into this trap is acute for academic educators, e.g. assigning a paper and formulating a research question, thereby telling students what to look for. To the extent that a preconceived conceptual filter is employed, it can block intuitive knowledge, silence tetchy questions, and thereby impede the discovery of newly critical knowledge.

The fall into this trap can come about through the use of words. They, of course, convey meanings. In Chapter 1, we began to consider the iconography of the term 'antiglobalization movement'. Going further, if resistance to globalization manifests at diverse sites, including in people's heads and cultural expressions (novels, plays, cartoons, etc.), why should resistance be put into a social-*movement* filter? And if resistance is an integral part of globalization itself, then it cannot be antiglobalization. Resistance is clearly inherent in global restructuring, which produces new winners and a multitude of losers, some of whose counter-actions coalesce into social movements while others do not. In short, antiglobalization is the wrong way to conceptualize resistance. Moreover, at present, with the rise of military globalization, resistance to globalization dovetails with peace marches that have used the networks and technologies mounted by global justice movements protesting globalization; these, in turn, were built on the anti-apartheid movement, IMF riots, the student revolts and the black-power movement of earlier decades, together with black and third-world feminisms, and Zapatista support networks.

In the teeth of military globalization, the term 'terrorism' has gained currency. The appropriation of this vocabulary varies according to the standpoints of the strong and the weak and along the spectrum of state-sponsored to nonstate terrorism. It is important to recall that the insurrectionists who took lives and property and attacked the colonial state during the American Revolution are known in the United States for their heroism and not decried as terrorists. During the anticolonial, armed struggle in Southern Rhodesia (today, Zimbabwe), the white minority regime and its supporters made frequent references to the 'terr war', but after the coming to power of a postcolonial state in 1980, the labeling of violence was reversed. Also, during the apartheid era, South Africa's white redoubt and President Ronald Reagan alike called the imprisoned Nelson Mandela a terrorist, but he later received the Nobel Peace Prize. Putting aside these discrepancies and exercising discursive power, President George W. Bush's wordsmiths have invoked the terrorism trope to pigeonhole quite diverse responses to domination, including elements of resistance to globalization.

To set the matter right, the intellectual resistance is in good part an ethical move. Whose words and voices are represented? Many neorealists and neoliberals paint pictures of globalization crises that touch down in Africa, Asia, and Latin America, and do so from the standpoint of the West or even just Washington, DC. For example, Robert Gilpin, a senior scholar whose work on the changing nature of global capitalism offers deep insights, derives his information on the Asian financial crisis mainly from Western sources, such as the Washington-based Institute for International Economics. Asian scholars, especially critical thinkers, are barely represented in Gilpin's chapter on 'Asian Regionalism' in *The Challenge of Global Capitalism* (2000), a basic text that has been widely adopted. The discussion of migration (Gilpin 2000: 295, 310) excludes the voices of migrants themselves, which could easily be tapped through interviews and other methodologies. In this case, one influential book among many, the subalterns are not permitted to speak.[3]

Whose voices, then, should be represented? By making this choice, the analyst necessarily integrates normative aspects of reflection in the account. There is no getting around it. The dilemma is that with multiple objects of study – a shifting and complex ontology – there must be a conceptual imposition. But who authorizes the interlocutor? What is the role of the interpreter? Is there a way to escape this dilemma?

The best way to cope is to make observations from standpoints along the range from the powerful to the powerless. Also, the globalization critic must be self-monitoring. The critic must listen, remain open, and make ample room for an array of voices from various zones, in a vertical and horizontal sense, in the globalization matrix. Epistemologically, the task is to elicit beliefs embedded in the agents' own consciousness about their conditions of existence and their notions of the good life. One must find out if the agents are actually suffering and frustrated, and explore what causes or explains the pain. In presenting evidence and plausible theorems, the globalization critic is not just observing what is out there but in part constructing propositions about hidden or subsurface phenomena, some of which may belie common sense (Geuss 1981).

The components of critical globalization studies

Building on the foregoing, a robust conceptualization of critical globalization studies would include the following complex of interacting components:

1   *Reflexivity* is an awareness of the relationship between knowledge and specific material and political conditions. To be reflexive is to probe historical beginnings and interests underpinning, or embedded in, a perspective or theory (Cox, R.W. 1986). A critical conceptualization of globalization warrants a searching consciousness of a series of transformations that constitute this set of processes.

2   *Historicism* incorporates the time dimension in globalization studies (Cox, R.W. 2002). It corrects the ahistorical approaches to globalization. For example, the common-sense notion that globalization is an inevitable force presupposes that it is a timeless essence without a beginning and an end. Rather, proceeding from definite historical locations, globalization is a distinctive configuration, with its own social power relations and whose future is open-ended. Thus, it is wrong to either engage in only presentism or collapse globalization into the vicissitudes of all world history. If globalization is historically constructed, then critical globalization studies requires rigorous historical thinking.

3   *Decentering* involves myriad perspectives on globalization from both its epicenters and the margins. Inasmuch as most globalization research is produced in the West, local knowledge elsewhere has the potential to generate distinctive discourses – on, say, Islamic globalization – and fresh questions. Indeed, aerial views of globalization require grounding. With its own specificity and contingencies, Africa surely offers an auspicious standpoint for entering the intricate dialectics of globalization and marginalization. This lens enables the critic to see globalization from the outside in.

4   *Crossovers* between the social sciences and complementary branches of knowledge are key to a critical understanding of globalization. Two types of crossovers are most pertinent: to other strands of critical theory, such as critical legal studies and critical cartography, and to real world problems, understood in a holistic manner. For example, to come to grips with the global HIV-AIDS pandemic and severe acute respiratory syndrome, or SARS, and the obstacles to mitigating these diseases, one must break disciplinary barriers. This approach involves a combination of medical, social, cultural, economic, and political research. Similarly, ecological renewal requires bridging social inquiry, humanistic studies, and the natural sciences.

5   *Strategic transformations* are about establishing counterhegemony: how to engage hegemonic power, upend it, and offer an emancipatory vision.[4] The

goal is to inculcate a new moral order in lieu of the dominant ethics – currently, an ethos of efficiency, competition, individualism, and consumption inscribed in neoliberalism. At issue, among other objectives, is democratic globalization, including accountability and self-determination. The means would require countervailing power (Chapter 8). At the end of the day, transformative action must have practical purposes.

The challenge is to excavate the above components of critical knowledge, examine their reciprocal interactions, and pull them together in a coherent whole. In other words, to cultivate critical globalization studies, conceptual interconnections must be strengthened.

A post-9/11 transformative agenda of studies

By any standard, September 11 was a cataclysmic event, but it did not herald the end of globalization, as some pundits hastily proclaimed (Gray 2001). Rather, 9/11 marked a restructuring of the processes that constitute globalization. Monumental violence, understood as an instrument of causes and interests, came to the fore. The political and military dimensions of globalization gained ascendance relative to its economic forces, often seen as the main root.

Post-9/11, there is a reconfiguration of global politics, with an opening of space. This is not necessarily a democratic opening, unless one thinks that free-market democracy is tantamount to substantive democracy. Rather, political space is increasingly occupied by nonstate actors, some of which are networks, such as Al Qaeda, with potential access to weapons of mass destruction. Perpetrated by transnational networks, hegemonic power, and 'rogue states', *militarized globalization* is a historical force defining our times. The corollaries are an enhanced role for police surveillance, as well as a we-ness and an othering promoted by the hegemonic power structure.

Presently, a transformative agenda of study would seek to explain the geo-strategic side of globalization and link it to the geoeconomic side as well as the biosphere.[5] It would explore the material structure of power that constitutes globalization. It would also examine resistances to globalization: not only the macro variants, like the battles of Seattle, but the micro-encounters, which manifest in the cultural sphere, and the several ways in which the macro and micro are mediated (Chapter 7).

How are these critical studies to be executed? The place to begin is thinking through the genesis of the contemporary order and then identifying the fault lines of power that would open up the possibilities for a transformation. The most conspicuous fault line today is the contradiction between globalization and unilateralism, which goes far beyond the historical pattern in US foreign policy of oscillation between engagement with and isolation from external forces. On the one hand, the US is the chief beneficiary of globalization. On the other hand, its political authorities, imposing the ideas of an ensemble of neoconservative organic intellectuals, the Christian right, and militarists, are undermining globalization.

Leading up to the 2003 Iraq war, the G.W. Bush administration refused to go along with its European allies and endorse the Kyoto Protocol on the environment, withdrew from the Antiballistic Missile Treaty with Russia, and challenged the accord banning landmines. The Bush team also flouted the International Criminal Court, refused to cooperate with Mexico on immigration, applied tariffs on steel in violation of international trade rules, approved an increase in subsidies to US farmers despite its lip service to lowering barriers to free trade, and told developing countries that it would not approve reducing the cost of life-saving drugs through exemptions from trade rules. In fact, with the backing of the American pharmaceutical industry, the US vetoed an agreement in the WTO, supported by the Europeans, that would have saved millions of lives. Meanwhile, when its allies in the Security Council threatened to veto US policy on Iraq, Washington criticized the use of the veto power and announced that it was prepared to go it alone. President Bush's decision to wage war also prompted a series of consumer boycotts of US icons such as Disney, McDonald's, and Coca-Cola, and aroused anti-American sentiment.

After the removal of Saddam, the Bush administration had to return to the UN Security Council to seek legitimacy, troops, and money, demonstrating that unilateralism does not preclude multilateral initiatives. US unilateralist policies contain elements of multilateralism partly because unilateralism is not in the interest of either American or global capital. Unilateralism is self-centered and adopts a short-run perspective, while the dominant fractions of capital are extroverted and take a longer view. Unilateralism, including the 2003 war in Iraq, is a retreat from the professed ideal of self-regulating globalization. To maintain a neoliberal world economy, multilateral political cooperation, at least among the principal actors, is needed. Overall, the trend suggests that a series of trade wars *and* military wars based on preemptive policies and, following Afghanistan and Iraq, 'regime change' may well constitute the next phase of globalization. In this sense, *unilateral globalization*, especially when militarized, is a quagmire if not an oxymoron. The two strands of *the new globalization* – unilateralism and free markets – are incommensurate.

In seeking out such contradictions, critical globalization studies requires research that probes embodied practices. This research can be carried out by networks of scholars and activists. Multi-sited and comparative research may provide diverse perspectives. Interregional and intraregional work illuminates the myriad ways in which globalization touches down and articulates with local conditions. Critical inquiry, including its pedagogy, is a means to a new common sense, and priority must be given to etching alternatives to the current order.

Desired knowledge

In sum, globalization studies is a highly contested domain, and there are no absolute lines for demarcating it. Within this broad compass, however, the distinctive province of a critical orientation is coming to be defined by a set of interrelated features: reflexivity, historicism, decentering, crossovers between social inquiry and other streams of knowledge, and transformative practices.

One advantage of a critical approach is that it offers a broad scope of knowledge. Although the institutions of organized power are major loci of globalization, it is also appropriate to consider informal and intersubjective processes (Cox, R.W. 2002).

Furthermore, critical globalization studies is a departure from other perspectives on globalization. Unlike economism, it does not underestimate agency, gender, mental frameworks, culture, and the environment. Unlike realism, it is not silent about social forces and the normative aspects of world order. Unlike neoliberal approaches to globalization, it does not focus on cross-border flows, interdependence, or technological advances as managerial problems and without linking them to hierarchic power relations and the structure of global hegemony.

It is one thing to distinguish critical globalization studies from related approaches, but does this mode of inquiry help to explain the transformations of our era? Critical globalization studies points to an interregnum that maintains elements of the old order, identifies continuities and discontinuities with the current order, and permits glimmers of a transition to a new order. I will call the old world order, *multilateral globalization*; the contemporary structure *militarized globalization*; and the potential constellation, *democratic globalization*. These three tendencies are not discrete and mutually exclusive alternatives. Their elements may co-exist as parts of a contradictory whole that embody varying aspects of globalization and different mixes of consent and coercion. While the first two tendencies are to varying degrees, driven by the US, the third is a counter to hegemonic globalization.

From the 1970s until 9/11, world order was based on a preponderance of consensus, especially among dominant classes, along with the periodic application of brute force. Built on a Westphalian model of formal equality among sovereign states, multilateral globalization embraced the principle of territoriality and the material capabilities of globalizing capitalism. The interstate system thus interacted with transnational processes, especially in the economic and cultural spheres. Not only has there been enormous structural inequality among the states themselves, but also globalizing markets produced increasing polarization among the rich and the poor, in some cases leading to heightened state repression, as in certain Middle Eastern countries. Emblematic of severe problems in the run-up to 2001 was a rapid rise in global environmental harms, including global warming, the hole in the ozone layer, and the loss of biodiversity.

Post-9/11, the pendulum in global hegemony swung from the side of consent toward coercion. Following the Asian financial crisis, the shock of market reforms in Russia and elsewhere, the Argentine debacle, and diminishing confidence in international economic institutions, the 'Washington consensus' needed reworking, as evidenced by sharp criticism from even some erstwhile pro-globalizers (Soros 2002) and neoclassical economists themselves (Rodrik 1997; and insiders such as Stiglitz 2002). Clearly, a more coerced, less consensual framework became ascendant. Washington increasingly relied on military power, covert agencies, and police force relative to more subtle forms of domination. Militarized globalization is characterized by both interstate war, notably in Iraq, and an erosion of the Westphalian system, with the territorial state facing mounting pressure from the disciplinary power of markets, regionalizing processes, and civil society (Falk 2003). The attempt to universalize American-led globalization has stimulated a surge in macro and micro resistance.

The resistance offers alternative futures, but they are more of a potential than a set of lived practices. There are many voices, sometimes at odds with one another; different visions; and no lack of concrete proposals (Sandbrook 2003). The centerpiece is a new normative architecture – an ethics based on concerns about social justice and equity. There are also calls to relax the Westphalian system without at all diminishing state capacity to regulate capital and strengthen social policies. In Polanyian terms, democratic globalization would re-embed the economy in society. And in a Gramscian sense, it is about building a counter-hegemony: an order that is tolerant of differences, seeks new ways to reconcile them in an open and participatory manner, and embraces a dispersion of power.

Currently, the three world orders intersect and compete, their different logics colliding with one another. The motor of transformation is not only countervailing power, but also alternative knowledge. It is neither metatheory nor a recipe for action. Rather, critical knowledge feeds on both contesting ideas and putting them into practice. The desired knowledge would provide intellectual tools to effect practical results. This should not be intellectually torturing, but demystifying and empowering. Critical globalization studies thus imagines and may be used to achieve a civilized future.

Having examined the cognitive structures that sustain or undermine the power of globalization, we are now in a position to consider their ideological representations. In the next part of this book, Chapter 5 focuses on the formulations of ideological leaders; Chapter 6 on the more latent ideology expressed at the base by members of civil society; and Chapter 7 on micro dimensions, the attitudes that are not always declared and relate, at least in part, to the realm of private, rather than public, life.

Part III

Ideology

5 Ideologies and the globalization agenda

If ideology is a way of looking at the world that justifies or undermines an existing order, then contemporary globalization must be viewed from different points on the hierarchies of power and privilege.[1] For those who hold power and possess wealth, globalization is an *ideology of freedom* for expanding not only the world's bounty but also human potential. At the other end of the power hierarchy, globalization is experienced as an *ideology of domination*, widening the divisions among humankind.

To varying degrees, these perspectives embrace a common element: a recognition of a dynamic of inclusion and exclusion. For example, James Wolfensohn, president of the World Bank, presents a vision shared by diverse observers who are rethinking the core ideas of globalization: '[O]ur challenge is to make globalization an instrument of opportunity and inclusion' (as quoted in Pfaff 2000). However, there is a tension between maintaining the dominant ideology and constructing counterideologies of globalization. Each current of ideology sets a different agenda – a broad program, not a detailed blueprint – for future world order. The objectives in this chapter are to identify these ideological clusters, delimit their varied globalization agendas, and critically evaluate them. It will be shown that complex ideologies of globalization are being reworked to fit a changing world order.

Approach

This chapter offers close textual analysis but does not explore the extent to which the evolved ideology and emergent counterideologies are actually embraced by the public in different contexts. Gauging latent ideologies of globalization requires empirical research – polling, interviewing, and surveys – and is the subject of the next chapter. In contrast, the emphasis here is on the transcripts of intellectual innovators. The focus is on ideological leadership in the sense that select ideas generated by intellectual visionaries are embodied in powerful institutions and transmitted through policy instruments. The ideas selected are never freestanding, but intimately related to political and material interests. When the outcome is an assertion of ideological hegemony, certain ideas become centerpieces of consensus, and consensus is more cost-effective than coercion.

The ideas infused in globalizing processes thus inform the exercise of power. Thought and action – theory and practice – are bound together so as to constrain and facilitate the possibilities for a social transformation. That said, ideological analysis helps to decipher codes of domination, identify the fault lines of power, and disclose efforts to form representations of counterpower. An ideological approach is useful insofar as it offers insight into the contested agendas for globalization.

As indicated, there is no monolithic doctrine of globalization. Uncertainties abound, there are ambiguities within ambiguities, and domination exists within domination. The consensual aspects, the ideological tonic, of hegemony are uneven, in flux, and in need of constant maintenance. With contemporary globalization, organic intellectuals not only produce new ideas but also make or challenge policy. In fact, intellectual participants in this process are linked in myriad formal and informal networks. These arrangements have a material dimension and may facilitate a broad, albeit uneven, consensus (Cox, R.W. 1979, 1996). Thus, in their respective and sometimes intersecting networks, organic intellectuals are not univocal but share basic values.

Within this range, a main axis is between the ideas framed at the center in North America and Europe and those at the margins. A heuristic that facilitates the examination of fluid blends, not a dichotomy, this distinction is only partly place-based and may be grasped in terms of the social relations of power. There are varied axes within the center and at the margins. While making allowance for these entanglements, it is clear that the views of globalization from the top substantially differ from the outlooks at the bottom. The late Claude Ake, one of Africa's leading intellectuals, presented a perspective from below: 'Marginalization is in reality the dynamics of globalization' (1996: 114). Indeed, the ideological thrust of globalization is begetting counterthrusts, albeit in embryonic forms. To explore these tendencies, I will first examine the core ideas embedded in the dynamics of neoliberal globalization and the extent to which they are implicated in public discourses.

The core ideas

Contemporary globalization is about neoliberalism, defined in Chapter 1 as both heightened integration in the world economy and a standard policy framework. As the *Financial Times* put it: '[Neoliberal g]lobalisation is merely the free market system on an international scale'. Further, 'the key is competition. . . . [Neoliberal globalisation] remains perhaps the most effective tool we have to make the world not just more prosperous, but also a freer and more peaceful place' (Paulson 2001). In another formulation, Gilpin weighs the views of the proponents of a neoliberal world economy and their critics who fear the consequences of market domination, and advances his own position: 'American political and security interests as well as economic interests are served by a united world economy' (2000: 348).

Rooted in classical political economy, neoliberalism may be traced to Adam Smith and others in this tradition. In the twentieth century, the free-market theories pioneered by philosopher-economist Friedrich von Hayek and his colleagues, including Milton Friedman, at the University of Chicago provided the intellectual underpinnings for the radical agendas of Thatcher and Reagan. These political leaders propagated neoliberal values, engineered the ideological shift from national Keynesianism to neoliberal globalization, and presented neo-liberalism as the generator of material well-being and rising productivity as the solution to social ills. They emphasized opening the market, not protecting society. Since the public sector does not compete for profits or market share, its scope, especially social spending, had to be reduced. To institute neoliberal ideas, there emerged the bedrock framework of deregulation, liberalization, and privatization.

A set of organizing institutions bundles neoliberalism and globalization, and seeks to universalize the core ideas. Among these diverse institutions are the media, the lecture circuit, schools, and universities, with business faculties being key to developing and disseminating neoliberal ideas. MBA programs serve as vital mechanisms in the transnational spread of a distinctive combination of values and hence for the emergence of a common ideological framework among policy-makers in several countries. Indeed, many MBA-toting ministers and senior bureaucrats around the world have been trained in neoclassical economics at leading universities in the US.

Also important in promoting a single dominant way of thinking about the world are bilateral and multilateral agencies, especially the WTO, the World Bank, and the IMF. Testimony to the interests served by international financial institutions is provided by Zbigniew Brzezinski, National Security Advisor to former President Jimmy Carter:

> [O]ne must consider as part of the American system of the global web of specialized organizations, especially the 'international' financial institutions. The International Monetary Fund (IMF) and the World Bank can be said to represent 'global' interests, and their constituency may be construed as the world. In reality, however, they are heavily American dominated and their origins are traceable to American initiative, particularly the Bretton Woods Conference of 1944.
>
> (Brzezinski 1997: 27)

Brzezinski adds that 'global cooperation institutions', i.e. the WTO, the World Bank, and the IMF, have established abroad major features of 'American supremacy' (1997: 28). Through policy mechanisms such as structural adjustment programs, international institutions have implemented the free-trade model and helped forge the 'Washington consensus', a framework for re-organizing economies and societies around neoliberal principles.

An initial incongruity in this ideology was the ascendance of state-led economies in Asia that did not adopt the path prescribed by neoliberal enthusiasts. Other anomalies, which appeared in rapid succession, were the debacle of 'shock therapy' market reforms in the former Soviet Union and parts of Eastern Europe, spectacularly the 1997–8 Asian economic crisis in which IMF advice contributed to the descending spiral, and the 2001 Argentine collapse wherein the neoliberal formula clearly accelerated the downturn. The cumulative impact of these experiences meant a loss of confidence in the 'Washington consensus'.

There have been various attempts to refurbish this consensus, such as the 2002 United Nations Conference on Financing for Development in Monterrey, Mexico. Toward this end, a complex of research institutions and think tanks in Washington, DC seek to advance discourses about public policy. The mission of these groups is to bridge public education and policy formulation. Also, leading public intellectuals who offer policy advice are propellants for new currents of ideological discourse.[2]

Ideological discourse

Let us now analyze exemplars of different sets of ideas and values about maintaining or undermining neoliberal globalization. Of course, no single exemplar completely typifies an approach, but the ones scrutinized below, to varying degrees, capture key features. The focus here is on four ideological currents: the centrist neoliberal school itself; leading criticism internal to this school – what may be called reformist neoliberal institutionalism; historical-materialist transformism; and development transformism. Although there are significant debates within each of these clusters, shared ideas are evident. The books considered in this chapter do not exhaust the range of possible ideologies and counterideologies.[3] My major concern is the ways in which these exemplar works frame agendas for globalization and alterglobalization.

1 *Centrist neoliberal thinking* is reflected in a World Bank Policy Research Report titled *Globalization, Growth, and Poverty: Building an Inclusive World Economy* (2000), a team project prepared under the supervision of Nicholas Stern, chief economist and senior vice president at the bank. In this study, the point of departure is that globalization corresponds to increasing integration of economies and societies throughout the world. The main contention is that in most cases, globalization reduces poverty and lessens inequality among countries though, on average, not necessarily within countries. The report emphasizes that globalization produces winners and losers within each society.

To sustain its arguments, this research demarcates three waves of globalization: 1870 to 1914, a period characterized by increasing cross-border flows – a time when globalization seemed 'inevitable'; 1950–80, years marked by greater integration among rich countries; and 1980 to the present, an age of rapid technological advance and a shift of manufactures to developing countries. With the third wave, 'the new globalizers' – also termed 'successful globalizers' – are beginning to catch up, and 'the less globalized' still face rising poverty. The report, rightly in my view, notes that there is no single model of success, thereby recognizing that the policy agendas must be custom-fitted. Disavowing nationalism and protectionism, the World Bank forthrightly states: '[T]here are no anti-global victories to report for the postwar Third World. We infer that this is because freer trade stimulates growth in Third World economies . . .' (2000: 37).

Following a series of chapters that focuses on economic phenomena, a penultimate chapter bracketing 'Power, Culture, and Environment' is inserted. There is discussion of 'the global institutional architecture' and the assertion that 'governments have many degrees of freedom to manage the interaction between trade, capital, and labor flows, on the one hand, and national culture and environment, on the other' (2000: 142). Not surprisingly, the prescriptions – the bank's agenda for globalization – give directions for improved market access.

On balance, this study signals a shift from the old orthodoxy. Among the important revisions in neoliberal thinking is a frank recognition of persistent marginalization concomitant to globalization, though, for the bank, marginalization is a descriptive statistical category, not a dynamic concept that turns on competing social forces. There is also acknowledgment that the state can provide elements of social protection; it may play an enabling role, as in the world's two most populous countries, China and India, both of which, in different ways, have sustained large-scale economic growth.

However, the premises of this report are open to challenge. In terms of historiography, are the first two waves really globalization? Or should they be construed as pre-globalization? If globalization is tantamount to world history, why employ the concept of globalization at all, and are the World Bank researchers trivializing it? Certainly the noneconomic relationships differ from one period to another (as from colonial rule to the postcolonial order).

While revisionist, is this neoliberal thinking resurrecting discredited modernization theories? In an era of globalization, to what degree is there autonomy for national policymakers, as the modernization thinkers posited? Further, do the neoclassical authors of this study regard the state as an invariant entity from 1870 to the present? More basically, is their basic supposition – globalization may be unidimensionally understood as economic integration – facile?

In light of the material infrastructure of their network, regular access to the world's leading political authorities, and the insinuation of ideas in the exercise of power, there can be little doubt that the 2000 World Bank Report is an important statement – one with great influence. It offers insight into corrections in the lens used by policymakers at the epicenter of globalization.

2 *Reformist neoliberals* take issue with centrist ideas and powerful institutions that convey them. These policy intellectuals participate in multiple networks: the lecture circuit, which goes along with quasi-celebrity status; the media industry; venues such as the WEF, where they interact with the top members of the corporate and political establishment; and research institutes at some of the world's highly endowed universities, which afford material support and are largely US-based. Noteworthy, however, is that a handful of leading economists, technically sophisticated masters of the neoclassical trade though not uniform in their views, such as Joseph Stiglitz, Dani Rodrik, Paul Krugman, and Jeffrey Sachs, have dissented from aspects of orthodox neoliberal globalization. Some of them collaborate in Stiglitz's Initiative for Policy Dialogue, a global network of social scientists established in 2000. Drawing together select experts from around the

world, its mission is to explore economic policy alternatives for developing and transition countries and to improve official decision making on economic issues.

A cabinet member in the Clinton administration (where he was chairman of the Council of Economic Advisers), then senior vice president and chief economist at the World Bank, winner of the 2001 Nobel Prize in economics, and now a professor at Columbia University, Stiglitz offers an insider's view into core institutions and ideas that drive the globalization agenda.

In *Globalization and Its Discontents,* Stiglitz (2002: 5) makes a case and provides evidence, e.g. on rising poverty in the world in the 1990s, somewhat at odds with data presented by the World Bank (cf. Stern 2000). In explaining why globalization does not work for a multitude of people, particularly in the developing world, Stiglitz constructs a multilevel analysis of globalization that focuses on economic integration, international economic institutions (especially the IMF, described as a 'political institution'), the interests of the financial and corporate community, state structures, social stratification, values, and the system of capitalism itself. Melding personal experience and theory in a skillful manner, Stiglitz lambastes the IMF for its hypocrisy and dogmatic adherence to the ideology of market fundamentalism. According to Stiglitz, the agenda should not be just to change the institutions themselves; the mind-sets about globalization and global governance warrant re-ordering.

Indeed, the case studies are revealing.[4] Stiglitz recounts the advice he personally rendered, the final decisions by political authorities, and the outcome of the heady events. In each instance, Stiglitz feels vindicated. He was right all along, and his ideas are not deemed to be ideology but elevated to the status of principle. In Stiglitz's mind, ideology takes on a pejorative connotation; it rigidifies thinking. What escapes notice is that ideology may also provide a critical understanding of the way in which a system operates, why it falls short of its goals, and what a just order might look like.

In terms of vision, Stiglitz calls for 'debt forgiveness', but why does he adhere to the tired concept of 'forgiveness' – after all, who owes what to whom? – rather than cancellation? His proposal for a 'multipronged system of reform' heaps together many different prongs and calls them a 'system'. In this 'system', the task is to *manage* problems. Presto, structural problems are reduced to management issues. Having criticized the market fundamentalists, Stiglitz then expresses his unshaken faith in the redeeming value of competition. At the end of the day, the agenda is to stabilize globalizing capitalism. It is to modify neoliberal globalization without tugging at the roots of its underlying structures.

3 *Historical-materialist transformers*, in marked contrast, have sought to reinterpret the ideas of capitalism and to restructure this globalizing system. Among others in this tradition, William K. Tabb, a professor at the City University of New York and long associated with the *Monthly Review* network and other circles of socialist scholars, has sought to extend Marxist understanding.

Pointing out that the media shape consciousness and provide 'an ideological context' for globalizing dynamics, his analysis nevertheless, and surprisingly, subscribes to some key representations in the public discourse, such as the notions of a 'global village' and an 'anti-globalization campaign' (Tabb 2001), which I sought to debunk in previous chapters. That said, however, Tabb – unlike the exemplar authors cited above – offers a vigorous critique of globalizing capitalism, and probes the very parameters within which national and international institutions operate.

Like the World Bank researchers and Stiglitz, Tabb is an economist, yet holds that neoliberal globalization is chiefly a political phenomenon. To develop his argument, Tabb takes a long view, as do Stern and his colleagues at the World Bank. But the authors at the bank historicize neoliberal globalization differently. After situating globalization in the development of capitalism, Tabb submits that there have been fundamental shifts since 1970, especially the end of the postwar era of national Keynesianism, the collapse of the Bretton Woods system of fixed exchange rates that accompanied the rise of the neoliberal regime, and the fall of the Soviet Union.

A historical-materialist perspective is structural in a way that the other worldviews are not. Tabb draws attention to the continuities between 'historical imperialism' and contemporary globalization. Further, he emphasizes structural power, i.e. imbalances not merely between lenders and borrowers, but the power relations among *both* states, including interstate institutions, and transnational classes. In short, Tabb's rethinking, and Stiglitz's as well, differ from the World Bank's inasmuch as Tabb and Stiglitz are decidedly reflexive on the interactions of ideas and interests.

From Tabb's perspective, the alterglobalization agenda is to bring an end to the 'form of indirect rule through global state governance institutions' – the WTO, World Bank, and IMF – and transnational corporations (TNCs). It is to effect an ideological shift toward the priorities of 'the emergent movement for global justice'. While supporting the importance of reform, the main idea in Tabb's analysis is to establish social control over market forces – a matter of transforming existing social relations.[5]

4 *Development transformism* is presented by Martin Khor, who, like the other exemplar authors, trained as an economist. He directs the Third World Network, a Malaysian-based NGO that works transnationally with other NGOs to understand and influence policy. His *Rethinking Globalization* (2001) focuses on the developing countries, many of them small and fragile actors that have experienced a reduction in policy latitude and an erosion of sovereignty (including over natural resources) and of local ownership in the national economy.

For Khor, globalization is not a totally new process, but one that has accelerated rapidly in the last few decades. He holds that a hallmark of this period is increasing inequalities among and within countries, and these divides are associated with globalizing forces. His data, drawn from United Nations Conference on Trade and Development and UNDP documents, thus contradict the World Bank's finding that there is not clear evidence for rising inequality among countries. According to Khor, globalization and the whole complex of ideas associated with the neoliberal framework have contributed powerfully to the vulnerabilities of the South. The mechanisms include loan conditionalities, fluctuations in commodity prices and terms of trade, and the volatility of short-term capital flows.

Based on this analysis, the agenda concerns protection against the policies and systemic risks of neoliberal globalization. Khor proposes strategic responses: *inter alia*, a selective policy of engagement with globalizing processes, a gradual pace, flexibility in choosing a policy mix, the identification of limits on external flows, and strong participation in establishing a regulatory framework. In this regard, he calls for strengthening the UN, including its specialized agencies, which have been marginalized by US unilateralist tendencies and faced by a tilt toward the WTO, World Bank, and IMF. A rebalancing of the state and the market would entail a recognition that they can be mutually reinforcing. Underpinning these ideas is the notion that if social justice and equity were to become a component of globalization, then democratic global governance could be on the agenda.

At the end of the day, the development perspective scrutinized here offers a vision that both converges with and diverges from aspects of the other ideological currents. Like the World Bank researchers and Stiglitz, Khor concentrates on the interactions between states (and interstate institutions) and markets. Unfortunately, in *Rethinking Globalization*, he is mostly silent about problems within the developmental state. The World Bank, Stiglitz, and Tabb, more than Khor, examine internal differences within countries. Unlike the World Bank researchers, Tabb peers into relational, not only gradational, divisions. He explores social relations, which Khor sets aside in favor of global imbalances. Surely these theoretical tools and frames of analysis are basic to the production of new knowledge about and representations of globalization.

Ideology in flux

In sum, neoliberal globalization may be grasped in terms of its intersubjective dimensions and transnational networks as they relate to political and material interests. Today, ideological consensus is increasingly contested and weakening. The fissures are widening. For diverse stakeholders, the challenge is to remake globalization into an *ideology of emancipation* for the many, not the few. Requisite to this task are not only new ideas but also countervailing power. Indeed, as demonstrated above, there is a substantial emergence of alternative sets of ideas: very different perspectives on a desirable globalization agenda. Ultimately, this contestation is a question of whose agenda will win out in the political strife. It comes down to a matter of reconciling core ideas and control of the globalization agenda.

Among the competing agendas, common ground exists, at least on one point: the contemporary era is marked by a bundling of neoliberalism and globalization. However, there is disagreement about what inference to draw from this convergence. Some ideologists clearly favor tightening the bundle, whereas others advocate an unbundling of neoliberalism and globalization. Indeed, what would globalization be like without neoliberalism?

Rethinking the debate over ideas thus shifts the globalization discourse from linking to delinking globalization and the neoliberal framework. Sequentially, delinking would be tied to relinking economic reform and social policy. But this dimension of alterglobalization is partial. The goal worth pursuing is to search for new philosophical principles that could help imagine options, guide policy, and inform strategies tailor-made for distinctive contexts. Even if there is no one best way to harness globalization so that it provides for both economic gains and social equity, surely much greater overall vision is still required. The vision would come from not only ideological leaders at the top but also from the base, where civil society is mounting pressure for alterglobalization.

6 'Common-sense' representations of globalization protests

(Co-authored with Glenn Adler)

Although the volume of literature on the ideology of globalization is rapidly proliferating (Rupert 2000; Steger 2000, 2003b), rigorous empirical and analytical studies on the many protests over globalizing forces are notably lacking.[1] In contrast, the media present vivid descriptions of these protests in major global cities on five continents. Popular writers also offer representations, an imagery, of the globalization protesters, who have become a regular feature of summits of world leaders, meetings of the major international economic institutions, and the venues of informal governance, such as the WEF. Together, these descriptions and imagery form 'common-sense' propositions, which we want to interrogate.

To study the globalization protests, scholars like Jackie Smith (2002) have drawn on participant observation, attendance at rallies and meetings of activists, informal interviews, and careful scrutiny of organizational literature and electronic communication, but have not systematically profiled the protesters. There are but few attempts by scholars, such as Ion Vasi (n.d.), to present a portrait of globalization protesters. More work has been done on the protesters contesting regionalization (Imig and Tarrow 2001). Empirical investigation of the globalizers is rich and suggestive (Sklair 1996; Rosenau *et al.* forthcoming); however, apart from first-hand accounts by several participants themselves, (Bové and Dufour 2000; Wallach and Sforza 2000; Barlow and Clarke 2001; Danaher 2001; Klein 1999, 2002), and a handful of more interpretive works (Ross 2003; Starr 2003), little detail is actually known about the protesters.

We want to find out: who are the globalization protesters? What are their socio-economic backgrounds? How do they conceive of themselves? What social criticism do they offer? Do the protesters form distinct groups, or is there fluidity and dispersion among members? Are the globalization protesters aligned to social movements? Are they prone to violence, ambivalent, or opposed to it? Exactly what do the protesters seek? Are they merely naysayers or also clearly for something?

The main purpose of this chapter is to examine an emergent concept of alterglobalization embraced by those who resist the dominant neoliberal construction. To do so, we first consider powerful mass-mediated representations of globalization protesters, and then explore pertinent theoretical issues. Next, to make clear our empirical account, we set forth the method adopted here and discuss its capabilities and limitations. Having listened to the voices of the resistance, we offer a case study of the April 2002 globalization protest in Washington, DC. On the basis of survey research, we indicate findings about the demography of the globalization protesters, their critique, their strategies and tactics for mobilization, and their goals for future globalization. Without totally erasing the distinction between audience and actors in social research, the former – our students – are invited to play a role in the production of new knowledge about globalization protests. Finally, our observations on the characteristics of the state of globalization protest are presented.

The production of media representation

Employing LexisNexis, various search engines, and all relevant search criteria (globaliz[s]ation, anti-globaliz[s]ation, WEF, WSF, and so on), we inspect the print media within a two-year period (October/November 2000–October/November 2002). We cover only mainstream English-language media: in the US, the *New York Times*, the *Washington Post*, and the *Wall Street Journal*; in the UK, *The Economist*, the *Financial Times*, and the *Guardian*; and in Southeast Asia, the *New Straits Times* (Kuala Lumpur) and the *Straits Times* (Singapore).[2] To supplement this sample of the mainstream print media, we also consider the images of globalization protesters in books by prominent journalists – works that help shape public opinion and play a role in the give-and-take of consensus formation. This survey will thus illustrate common representations of the protesters, and is meant to be a pointer for future research.

Notwithstanding the caveats entered above, a sketch of prevailing representations includes a set of recurrent images that comes into view with great frequency. Numerous interviews with protesters convey their appearance, ages, gender, national origin, educational and social status (university student, middle class, etc.), and organizational affiliation (Black Bloc, Anti-Capitalist Convergence, ATTAC, and so on). The protesters are portrayed as predominantly young, white, educated, and middle class. They are typically categorized under the omnibus label 'antiglobalization' activists or movement.

That said, another imputed characteristic of the globalization protesters is discord among the protesters themselves. Considerable attention is given to the differences between the globalization protesters and trade unionists, especially in the US (*Financial Times* 2 May 2002). The former are reportedly concerned about issues such as sweatshops, debt, fair trade, the environment, and human rights, whereas the trade unions especially want to protect their members' jobs. In this connection, the media repeatedly pose the question, Who represents whom?

> The meeting in Qatar also has underlined some of the awkward divisions between the anti-globalization forces and the governments of poor nations whose interests the activists purport to champion. Although the activists and the developing countries take the same position on some issues, such

as the desirability of easing international drug patent rules, they differ
sharply on others.

(*Washington Post* 12 November 2001)

In this imagery, again frequently found in the newspapers, the globalization
protesters and those who represent developing countries have discrepant priorities
and even clash.

A third putative attribute is a propensity for violence. This is hardly surprising
in light of the property damage and confrontation with police at the 1999 Seattle
demonstration and subsequent globalization protests, as well as the violence
perpetrated by police, including the killing of a protester in Genoa, Italy in 2001.
The *New York Times* has not been alone in constructing images like the 'chaos that
accompanied last year's summit meeting in the quiet, snowcapped mountains of
Davos, Switzerland, or the violence that swirled at the World Trade Organization
meetings in Seattle and Genoa' and the 'wild protest melees at Seattle and Genoa'
(*New York Times* 11 January 2002 and 25 January 2002). Surely following the
September 11 terrorist attacks, it is no wonder that the potential for violence
became a central concern. Immediately after 9/11, the protesters de-emphasized
confrontation, as reported in the mainstream print media. Yet several newspaper
articles continued to take a broad-brush approach in associating protesters with
violence and conjuring up images of anarchy as 'chaos', but not direct democracy,
transparency, and community self-determination, which is what anarchists claim
that they stand for.

A fourth trait is incoherence. Not mincing its words, *The Economist* describes
the goals of the protesters as being 'too absurd' and their arguments as 'too
incoherent' (*The Economist* 28 September 2002). In less dismissive language, other
mainstream print media dwell on a lack of cohesive detail for changing global
practices and international institutions. Writing in a popular venue, Columbia
University economist and public intellectual Jagdish Bhagwati similarly portrays
the protesters as being unaware of the benefits of capitalism and simply
uninformed about globalization and corporations (Bhagwati 2002). This
representation of protesters is of a multitude without vision of alternatives. From
a different angle, in the wake of the 1997–8 Asian financial crisis, the mainstream
newspapers in Malaysia and Singapore are aware that their leaders have spoken
loudly against aspects of globalization, e.g. unregulated transfers (known as 'hot
money') in and out of developing countries. Hence, the representation of what
the protesters are against is 'unfettered globalization', with recognition that
the protests are about 'refining globalization' – not total rejection (*Straits Times*
1 February 2002).

Embellishing these representations of the globalization protesters, books by
leading Western journalists have disseminated the same images. *New York Times*
correspondent Thomas Friedman portrays globalization protesters as 'backlashers'
and doubts that a coherent ideological response to globalization will develop
(Friedman, T. 1999: 273). John Micklethwait and Adrian Wooldridge focus on the
potential for violence and the 'more sinister agenda' of a 'disenfranchised, angry

minority with a minimal grasp of economics' (Micklethwait and Wooldridge 2000: 274–5). The crossover between journalists and scholars like Bhagwati and other public intellectuals who fashion galvanizing metaphors is particularly apparent. For example, although he is but one of many who has used this metaphor, social theorist Anthony Giddens, an advisor to UK Prime Minister Tony Blair, has likened globalization to 'a runaway world'. The theme of his prestigious BBC Reith Lectures in 1999 and the title of one his books, *Runaway World*, does indeed capture the lack of control in contemporary world order and the unprecedented ways in which technological forces are speeding our lives (Giddens 2000). True, a runaway may not have a rider, but surely there are power relations – a hierarchy – between a rider, or actually riders, and a horse. In fact, the runaway encounters fences and efforts to rein it in. Today, states, international organizations, and resistance movements alike seek to tame the runaway horse. The point is that with contemporary globalization, serial characteristics and popular metaphors help to order complex and multidimensional phenomena but risk obfuscating deeper structures.

To recap, the power of mainstream media representation, aided by certain scholars and public intellectuals, produces four popular images of globalization protesters: youthful and middle class, violence-prone, divided, and lacking coherent positions. Our research tests this template against survey data, but first it is important to consider a more general question: what theoretical issues are at play here?

Theoretical issues

Our analysis rests on the premise that globalization is animated by not only a surge in global flows but also fundamental power relations involving both maintenance of the dominant order and impulses for resistance to it (Chapter 1). As with the Zapatistas, local grievances are combined with discontents over globalizing processes, be they structural adjustment programs, privatization, deregulation, or liberalization. The globalization protests are linked to prior popular protests over policies that are perceived as harming the interests of the poor and dispossessed. Hence, as indicated, a series of IMF riots on three continents mobilized large numbers of people in the developing world (Walton and Seddon 1994; McMichael 2004). Protest movements have also stopped illegal logging, often by TNCs, and megaprojects such as large dams. In addition, the failed campaign to defeat NAFTA in the early 1990s contributed to public consciousness about the promises and limitations of state-supported market integration. Current protests tap this consciousness. Contemporary globalization protests build on and intensify local tendencies to redress grievances, which run deep in some historical contexts.

Inasmuch as contemporary globalization unsettles old solidarities based on nation and state, today's protests are about the construction of new collective identities that increasingly transcend territorial units. The old senses of community are less secure. There are shifts in identity politics, with the affirmation of multiple identities, including class, gender, sexual orientation, religion, and race and ethnicity. In fact, alterglobalization thrives on this explosion of pluralism.

Thus, the globalization protests are partly about ideological understandings of shifts in the global political economy. The expressions of the protesters themselves are not necessarily the same as the more nuanced views of ideological leaders. Rather, the swell in the streets bears the more *latent* and fluid attitudes at the base. The street protests register attempts to reconcile ideology and new policy agendas – adjustments in the strategies of international economic institutions, efforts to forge a post-'Washington consensus', and especially the emphasis by the US and its allies on fighting global terrorism. It cannot be overemphasized that at issue is a dynamic process of joining ideology and transformations in both geoeconomics and geopolitics.

In the scholarly literature, there are overlapping approaches for investigating these tendencies. One is to focus on the interactions between globalization and 'antiglobalization' movements. In this genre, a sophisticated effort is David Held and Anthony McGrew's *Globalization/Anti-Globalization* (2002). This concise book probes the changing geography of capitalism, the spatial organization of power, state and societal security, and guiding ethical principles. It encapsulates a structural and agential analysis in a single framework. But there is a problem of voice. Nowhere in this book are the losers in contemporary globalization permitted to speak in their own voices. The authors have contributed importantly to understanding globalization, yet they choose not to incorporate empirical referents on the protesters in their study. By doing so, one could capture the multiple shadings on spectra that range from embracing facets of neoliberal globalization to wanting to reform or abolish it. One could also gauge the intensity of such positions. This, of course, reaches beyond and below actually solidified movements seeking to bring about collective action and would enable the researcher to look for potential for transformation.

Globalization-from-below, according to Richard Falk (2003), signals a new sort of politics – a civil-society activism on display at the 1999 Seattle demonstrations and subsequent street protests. Heterogeneous and diverse, the bottom–up initiatives stand for a participatory and democratic globalization. They are opposed to the top–down, hierarchical politics embodied in state and corporate entities. Setting up a heuristic, not a binary separation, Falk has deepened the debates by incorporating normative politics; but, again, we would also like to hear directly from the standpoint of those at the bottom and know precisely how they frame their contentions.

By all means, bottom-up initiatives do not arise easily. Faced with similar threats generated by globalization, not all individuals or groups are moved to collective action. The range of opportunities to engage in protest matter, as do the resources people have at their disposal, the traditions of resistance upon which they can draw, and the social networks in which they are embedded. For the last two decades, these issues have been the core concerns of social-movement theory. Yet only since the late 1990s have scholars in this field made important contributions to understanding the development of transnational solidarity and its impact on global governance (Smith, Chatfield, and Pagnucco 1997; Keck and Sikkink 1998; O'Brien *et al.* 2000).

This social-movement research is not without its problems. Sidney Tarrow (2002) has criticized the literature's underspecification of the causal links between globalization and collective action, and its lumping together of myriad forms of collective action. He has proposed examining transnational collective action within the broader framework of 'contentious politics', as advanced with his co-authors (McAdam, Tarrow, and Tilly 2001). This framework aims at overcoming both the static approach of standard social-movement analysis and the limits to generalization imposed by relying too heavily on the case-study method. 'Contentious politics' stresses the ways in which movements attribute threats and opportunities, appropriate organizational sites, develop cognitive frames, and innovate collective action (Tarrow 2002: 241–5). The 'contentious politics' approach makes many contributions to social-movement theory and is complementary to our research. However, it has not yet advanced understanding of the empowering or disempowering workings of globalization, for the analysis is not sufficiently tied to the vicissitudes of a globalizing economy.

In alerting us to the ways in which transnational collective action is at all possible, social-movement theory – and its 'contentious politics' variant – identifies as well its fragility. The coalition that mobilized for the 'Battle of Seattle', for instance, is rife with tensions. According to Mark Lichbach (2002), these include differences among groups' material interests, identities, and ideals; between groups from the North and the South; and over their tactics.[3] That these differences were mitigated in Seattle is not to say that globalization protests will cohere in a sustained, global social movement. Scholars have pointed to the possibility – post 9/11 – of the renationalization and narrowing of the global justice movement's agendas as they are reconfigured in response to 'resurgent hegemonic nationalism' (Ayres and Tarrow 2002: 3).

The range of phenomena addressed under the umbrella of 'contentious politics' is far broader than the scope of this chapter. We focus on a discrete instance of globalization protest that made claims on international economic institutions and the US state over a number of 'days of action' in April 2002. For our purposes, the most useful construct is resistance, understood as an integral part of globalization itself.

In Chapter 2, it was shown that resistance is not merely a negation. Resistance is more than opposition, evasions, challenges, or reactions. It is constituted by and constitutive of globalization. Resistance involves new ideas, organizations and institutions, daily practices, and a plurality of dispersed, local, and personal points of counterpower (Gills 2000; Mittelman 2000). The degree to which each of these dimensions is present or absent under different conditions can provide the basis for comparative inquiry. This multifaceted approach adds to the interpretations layered above, and helps to order the data analyzed in the pages that follow.

Method

Our main findings derive from a survey conducted during one of many protests in Washington, DC, during the weekend of 19–22 April 2002. A coalition of national organizations called the actions to protest the policies of the World Bank and the IMF, as well as of the US, principally regarding the Israeli–Palestinian conflict.

Before administering the survey questionnaire (see Appendix), we held two sessions to involve students in producing the instrument and to discuss procedures and ethical issues. Just as the protestors engaged in a learning process, students helped shape the research. They contributed to designing the questionnaire, provided an archive of first-hand accounts of protests, bore witness to resistance, and became agents in knowledge production. Without exaggerating the scope of the undertaking, the parallel process among protestors and students may be regarded as a double pedagogy.

The survey polled participants at the 20 April rally sponsored by the Mobilization for Global Justice at Edward R. Murrow Park, located opposite World Bank headquarters. With between 1,000 and 5,000 participants in attendance, the event culminated in a march, which merged with protests from three other actions, and a rally at the Mall attended by between 75,000 and 100,000 protesters (*Los Angeles Times* 21 April 2002; *Washington Post* 21 April 2002; *Washington Times* 21 April 2002).

The fieldwork carried out by 12 students and two professors yielded 243 completed questionnaires.[4] Each questionnaire contained 25 items, covering demographic features, participation in previous protests, attitudes toward globalization, and the strategies of the global justice movement.

The limitations to the research stem from the decision to survey participants while the protest was in progress. These drawbacks concern the representativeness of the sample, the validity of certain findings, and the generalizability of the results.

The interviewees were not chosen through strict random sampling because of the impossibility of generating a sampling frame. Rather, the student field researchers were asked to diversify their selection of interviewees, based on a number of identifiable characteristics, such as gender, race, and age. Moreover, the rally's dispersion created selection problems. The bulk of the questionnaires were administered at Murrow Park, although some interviews were conducted along the protest route, and in some instances, at the rally site on the Mall. This sample may include participants from other rallies whose principal reason for attendance was not the global justice movement but related issues that served as focal points for protest that day. This may influence certain findings, such as the participants' view that US foreign policy – as opposed to issues more specifically pertaining to the IFIs – was their primary reason for attending. However, inasmuch as the rallies were jointly coordinated, flowed into each other, and overlap in activists' membership in allied movement organizations, we decided to tally all the completed questionnaires.

Time limitations on each interview prevented probing more deeply into certain issues, and validity problems may have been introduced. For example, interviewees were asked whether key features of globalization were a benefit or cost for ordinary people. When given opportunities to comment on the questionnaire, some interviewees criticized the either/or choice, preferring to construe globalization as having a differentiated impact depending on geography (global North and global South), or the class of the person affected. In many, though not all, cases in which items dealt with nuanced issues, we provided open-ended questions to allow interviewees to expand on their answers.

Finally, the survey research concentrated on a single rally, and did not examine preparations for the protest, interactions among groups, or the dynamics of the event itself. The survey provides a degree of concreteness and accuracy that would not otherwise be possible. Needless to say, these results are not taken to be the attitudes of all globalization protestors in the US, much less the world, nor is it assumed that street rallies are more important than other forms of protest. What is gained by centering on a specific event, however, is limited by the difficulties of generalizing about the development of globalization protests. To be sure, these constraints are not reasons for discarding survey research, but suggest the need to extend the use of surveys and combine them with other methods to understand protest dynamics.

Findings[5]

Demography

Protesters from 20- to 24-years-old make up the largest single age group, accounting for nearly 36 per cent of the sample. More than one-third of the sample is over 30 years old, and more than 20 per cent is over 40.[6] In addition, 52 per cent of the interviewees are male; 48 per cent, female. Overall, the protesters are highly educated. Sixty per cent either attended or completed college, and nearly 25 per cent enrolled in or finished graduate school. More than 6 per cent had earned a PhD. Less than 2 per cent had a technical degree or certificate.

Although the bulk of the interviewees – more than 40 per cent – identify themselves as students, the sample is more occupationally diverse than this finding suggests. Over one-third of the interviewees are employed as professionals or in an executive, managerial, or administrative capacity. However, the class composition is not diverse. Only 2 per cent are clerical workers; 6 per cent, craftsmen or manual laborers; and less than 2 per cent are unemployed.

Forty-one per cent report household income of under $25,000, and nearly 30 per cent indicate household income of $50,000 or more. The correlation between household income and education is statistically significant, showing that income is more likely a function of the interviewees' education level than of class position. In other words, the household income results demonstrate that there were large numbers of high school and college students under the age of 20 and not a substantial presence of poor people.

While 80 per cent of the interviewees self-identify as US or Canadian citizens, another 5 per cent hold dual US citizenship. Participation from beyond North America is greater than in other protests.[7] Although a large majority of the sample is white, almost 30 per cent regard themselves as members of minority groups. However, given the number of foreign citizens for whom the term 'minority' may not carry racial connotations, the relatively large proportion of minority-group members does not reflect racial diversity per se.

The interviewees are generally cosmopolitan. Forty-four per cent speak two or more languages. Nearly half (48 per cent) travel abroad once each year or more. More than 90 per cent regularly use email to contact people in other countries, and almost 30 per cent frequently communicate by email with more than ten people in foreign countries.

Critique of globalization

The questionnaire contains a number of items that explore the interviewees' views about globalization and the key policies and institutions with which it is associated.

Asked to evaluate the effects of globalization, 88 per cent of the interviewees not surprisingly believe that globalization has a direct impact. Of the 88 per cent, two-thirds say that globalization diminishes the quality of their lives. However, a small but notable minority (19 per cent) claim that globalization enhances the quality of life, with 14 per cent of the sample replying 'don't know'. This again points to complicated views about the effects of globalization, as Table 6.3 demonstrates. It records responses concerning the impact of attributes of global-ization and their consequences for everyday life. (Here and in other tables, the total percentage is rounded to 100.)

Interviewees consider altering local cultures, reducing government expenditure, and privatization in almost uniformly negative terms. Yet other dimensions of globalization yield more mixed responses. While three-fifths of those surveyed see export promotion as a cost, 14 per cent deem it a benefit, and 19 per cent are unsure. Interviewees assess migration, greater availability of consumer goods, and technological advances in increasingly positive terms. Nearly half (46 per cent) regard technological advances as a benefit, and 21 per cent are uncertain. These findings clearly suggest that interviewees think that globalization is not a monolith, and readily differentiate the impact of its constituent processes.[8]

Interviewees were also surveyed about their views concerning the impact of various international organizations and transnational corporations on ordinary people. Whereas interviewees register some unfamiliarity with certain institutions, such as international security and regional organizations, the attitudes expressed are extremely consistent. Nearly three-quarters believe that NGOs have a very positive or positive effect on ordinary people, while only 6 per cent see NGOs as having a very negative or negative effect. The only other organization to receive a majority positive response is the UN. Regional organizations, such as the EU, are perceived in more mixed terms, with a plurality rating them as either very positive/positive or not having much effect. In comparison, TNCs, international security organizations, such as NATO, and international economic institutions, including the WTO, the IMF, and the World Bank, are consistently assigned negative rankings. With their responses ranging from 89 per cent to 93 per cent,

Table 6.1 'Does globalization affect you personally?'

	Per cent
Yes	88
No	5
Don't know	6
Missing	1
Total	100

Table 6.2 'On balance, how does globalization affect the quality of your life?'

	Per cent
G enhances my quality of life	19
G diminishes my quality of life	66
Don't know	14
Total	100

Table 6.3 'Here's a list of features associated with globalization. Do you think these are benefits or costs for ordinary people in the world?' (per cent)

	Benefit	Cost	Don't know	Missing	Total
Altering local cultures	0	89	7	4	100
Reduce government spending	5	89	4	3	100
Privatization	5	83	9	3	100
Export promotion	14	61	19	7	100
Increasing migration	18	50	26	7	100
Greater availability of consumer goods	23	44	25	8	100
Technological advances	46	26	21	7	100

Table 6.4 'Do you believe that, on balance, the following institutions have a positive or negative effect on ordinary people in the world?' (per cent)

	NGOs	UN	Regional orgs	Security orgs	WTO	IMF	World Bank	TNCs
Very positive or positive	73	54	25	8	3	3	3	1
Neutral	11	28	21	11	3	3	2	3
Very negative or negative	6	14	29	71	89	90	90	93
Don't know	10	5	25	11	5	5	5	3
Total	100	100	100	100	100	100	100	100

Table 6.5 Institutions' effects on ordinary people (per cent)

	World Bank	WTO	IMF	TNCs
Negative	27	16	17	21
Very negative	63	73	73	72

those surveyed think that these organizations have either a negative or very negative effect on ordinary people. Further evidence that these views are strongly held is that few of the interviewees are unsure about their responses: consistently, 5 per cent or less indicate 'don't know'.

Disaggregating the results shows that the interviewees hold differentiated attitudes toward these organizations. Those surveyed see the World Bank's impact on ordinary people in less negative terms than the others, insofar as less than two-thirds, as opposed to nearly three-quarters for the WTO, IMF, and TNCs, view the bank in very negative terms. The responses regarding the WTO (73 per cent), IMF (73 per cent), and TNCs (72 per cent) are about the same; however, when one totals negative and very negative scores, TNCs are seen as having the worst impact on the lives of ordinary people. The consistency of these negative findings suggests that the interviewees regard the WTO, IMF, and TNCs as integral components of globalization.

Taken together, the results show reinforcing views about globalization. On the one side, the interviewees tentatively embrace (or are at least less negative toward) a number of major aspects of globalization – the promise of technological advance, increased migration, and greater availability of consumer goods. Nevertheless, time and again they worry about key policies associated with globalization, such as privatization, export promotion, and reductions in govern-ment expenditure. Not surprisingly, the interviewees disapprove of the central institutions that advocate and implement the dimensions of globalization deemed most problematic.

Mobilization, goals, strategy

A Mobilization

In order to gauge levels of political commitment, the questionnaire calls for information on how interviewees traveled to the protest. Is participation situational – comprised of locals with easy access to the site – or does protest entail more deliberate planning? The results indicate that attendance is more often the product of considerable calculation: 56 per cent of the interviewees travel more than 100 miles to demonstrate, while only 38 per cent travel less than 50 miles. More than 10 per cent come from more than 1,000 miles away.

Also, the Internet is an important factor shaping participation. First, we surveyed use of the Internet as a means for networking with like-minded people.

Table 6.6 'How frequently have you used the following forms of the
Internet to gather information about these protests?' (per cent)

	Web sites	Chatrooms	Listservs	Email
Often	65	5	48	69
Sometimes	28	6	28	23
Never	6	87	22	7
Don't know	1	2	1	2
Total	100	100	100	100

More than 80 per cent of the interviewees do so on a regular basis – one or more times per week – and more than half (55 per cent) do so on a daily basis. Only 5 per cent of the interviewees never use the Internet for this purpose.

A follow-up question delved into the ways in which interviewees use electronic communication to gather information about the protests. The most common means is by accessing a Web site, as do 93 per cent of the interviewees. Seventy-six per cent collect information through a listserv, a more interactive form of electronic communication in which participants share enough in common and have sufficient competence to arrive at the venue. Only a small proportion (11 per cent) use chatrooms to learn about the protest.

In response to a separate question, more than two-thirds of the interviewees say that information gathered on the Internet actually influences their desire to participate in a protest, and only 11 per cent report that such information does not influence their decision.

These results roughly parallel those reported by Vasi (n.d.: 19), who surveyed a demonstration held during the September 2001 World Bank/IMF meetings in Washington, DC. The Internet plays an important mobilizing role in both protests, given the mainstream media's selective coverage of the events; however, the percentage of people who gather information on the Internet and the percentage who claim that it influences their decision to participate are higher in our sample. Although the finding is weak, the correlation between organizational activism and the influence of information obtained on the Internet is statistically significant and negative, indicating that the importance of the Internet as a mobilizing tool diminishes as a participant's degree of activism increases.

While seasoned activists are likely to be influenced by interpersonal and organizational factors, non-members in a social movement or those without protest experience are apt to rely on the Internet as an effective bridge to mobilization. This finding suggests the emergence of 'virtual protest organizations' resulting in 'increased movement participation of civic-minded individuals' (Vasi n.d.: 20).

By asking interviewees to identify their role in social movements, including global justice, labor, environmental, antinuclear, peace, civil rights, gay and lesbian, and other organizations, we created an index based on the extent of their participation: non-involvement, inactive or active membership, or officeholder.[9]

Table 6.7 Correlation between Internet influence on the decision to participate and degrees of organizational participation in social movement organizations

			Internet influence	*Degrees of organizational participation*
Kendall's tau *b*	Internet influence	Correlation coefficient	1.000	−0.177(*)
				0.001
		Sig. (2-tailed) *N*	239	239
	Degrees of organizational participation	Correlation coefficient	−0.177(*)	1.000
			0.001	
		Sig. (2-tailed) *N*	239	243

* This correlation is significant at the 0.01 level (2-tailed).

Table 6.8 'Are you involved in any of the following movements' organizations?' (Degree of participation in movement organizations)

	Number	*Per cent*
Very active	27	11
Active	50	21
Moderately active	100	41
Passive	64	27
Total	241	100

Table 6.9 'Are you involved in any of the following movements' organizations?' (Number of movement organizations in which involved)

	Number	*Per cent*
None	66	27
One	27	11
Two	32	13
Three	41	17
Four or more	77	32
Total	243	100

Table 6.10 'Have you participated in any of the following global justice protest activities?' (Degree of participation in global justice protests)

	Number	*Per cent*
Very active	15	6
Active	51	21
Moderately active	47	19
Passive	130	54
Total	243	100

The results demonstrate that nearly three-quarters of the interviewees claim some connection to a movement organization. A substantial core of the protesters – nearly one-third – are activists in a movement organization. Indeed, many interviewees are involved in more than one organization: nearly one-third in four or more. This pattern marks a substantial exchange between organizations, which further suggests the possibility of interaction in terms of broad goals, strategies, and tactics.

However, the focus on the activists should not obscure another key feature of the interviewees' organizational participation. More than two-thirds of those involved in the protest are not drawn from this activist core. Forty-one per cent are only moderately active in one or more movement organizations, while more than one-quarter of the participants are in fact not involved in such organizations at all. These results differ from those reported by Vasi (n.d.: 26), who found that all respondents in his sample were involved in more than one movement. Our results indicate that the organizers of the April 2002 action are able to reach out beyond their own activist ranks to draw in less active members as well as a large group of individuals previously uninvolved in organizations. Far from being an assembly of the converted, the protest motivated large numbers of marginal members and the uninitiated into protest activity. These results are especially striking in light of the sensitivity surrounding popular protest after 9/11.

The significance grows when seen through the lens of the participants' prior involvement in protest. On the basis of surveying interviewees about a number of different events, ranging from the 1999 WTO protest in Seattle to the September 2001 World Bank/IMF demonstration in Washington, DC, we constructed an index of the interviewees' degree of participation in previous protests.[10]

If three-quarters of the protesters have at least some form of organizational involvement, nearly the same number – 73 per cent – are at most moderately engaged in global justice protest action. In fact, more than half – 54 per cent – never previously participated in such protests. Not only are the protesters drawn from beyond an activist core, they are also largely individuals who are relatively new to global justice protest activities. Although the overall numbers involved in the Murrow Park rally are small, especially compared to past global justice protests, the organizers' ability to attract newcomers at a time of national anxiety about protest points to potential for expansion of the movement.

B Goals

The question about the most important reason for joining the protest included explicit options that distinguish among competing strategic goals in the global justice movement. When asked in this manner, only 6 per cent of the interviewees identify abolition of IFIs as the major reason for joining the protest. Another 20 per cent choose reforming IFIs. The largest single response (42 per cent) is 'to oppose current US foreign policy'. A smaller number – 18 per cent – say that protesting capitalism is the main reason for participating in the event.

Table 6.11 'What is the most important reason
that you are here today?'

	Per cent
Abolish IFIs	6
Reform IFIs	20
Protest capitalism	18
Oppose US foreign policy	42
Other	14
Total	100

It is striking that when given a clear choice, only a small proportion associate with the 'abolitionist' position. However, the way of framing the question risks misrepresenting participants' views. In fact, the options are not completely discrete alternatives; pushing people to choose between them may obscure important interconnections. Thus, an open-ended item allowed interviewees to elaborate their answers. Those who did so indicate more complex thinking about choices than is usually reported in the debates about the global justice movement's objections to IFIs.

Many protesters believe that both the reformist and abolitionist positions are bound up with a broader protest against capitalism and US foreign policy. While a small number interpret this protest in the binary categories of reform or revolution, most describe their reasons in terms of overall ends, not means. In the voice of one protester: 'I want a world without economic/political/social coercion'. Other interviewees emphasize curtailing or challenging corporate power, and including environmental concerns in economic decision-making. One answer, which captures the theme of a number of responses, stresses a '[c]ampaign for a democratic, just and ecologically sane economy'.

The majority of these open-ended responses posit a connection between corporate power and capitalism. As one interviewee puts it, the issues are inseparable since the industrial capitalist economies are the 'primary agent[s]' of globalization. In the same fashion, many perceive globalization as inseparable from the vicissitudes of US foreign policy. Far from regarding state power as diminishing as a result of globalization and yielding sovereignty to TNCs or IFIs, these interviewees look at the US state as an active, interventionist agent of globalization. The focus on the US state provides a link between the traditional concerns of the global justice movement and those animating emergent protests against the US role in the Middle East, Colombia, and Afghanistan. This combination of views helps explain the rapid merger on 20 April of globalization protests against the World Bank and the IMF with the large rally for Palestinian rights.

Given an opportunity to develop their answers, the interviewees mention sweatshops, debt, and human rights, but not trade and protectionism – positions imputed to many in the US global justice movement. This silence about trade

Table 6.12 'What is your response to the following statement:
"Violence is a legitimate strategy in protesting globalization"?'

	Per cent
Agree strongly	4
Agree	16
Neither agree nor disagree	7
Disagree	17
Disagree strongly	47
Don't know	1
Refuse	6
Total	100

and protectionism may be partly attributable to the absence from the April 2002 protests of the American Federation of Labor–Congress of Industrial Organizations, which, along with its many affiliates, had been substantially involved in previous globalization protests. However, nearly 30 per cent of the interviewees identify themselves as participants in the labor movement, as officers or ordinary members.

C Strategy

If the protesters are diverse in terms of their previous involvement in global justice demonstrations and their degree of activism, and subscribe to varied and complicated views about the movement's goals, so do they hold a range of attitudes about the movement's strategies.

Asked about violence as a strategy, nearly two-thirds of the interviewees exclude it as a legitimate means to protest globalization. Nonetheless, it is noteworthy that at a demonstration dedicated to 'peace and justice', more than one-fifth of the interviewees indicate that violence is a legitimate strategy. While this result should not be overstated – only 4 per cent agree strongly that violence is legitimate and 47 per cent strongly disagree – the data again show the complexity of the protesters' views.

Three-fifths of those surveyed responded to an open-ended question on violence. A strong plurality of them rule out violence under any circumstances, invoking the names of Mahatma Gandhi and Martin Luther King Jr. or a religion (Christianity, Buddhism, and the Society of Friends) to justify their positions. In this reading, the global justice movement poses a moral critique of globalization and demarcates the parameters of acceptable protest.

Other interviewees strongly repudiate violence but for pragmatic reasons. They believe that whether or not violence is morally justified, its use would jeopardize the movement by giving it bad publicity. For some, what they construe as legitimate uses of violence would most likely be negatively portrayed in the media and thereby diminish the movement's effectiveness by alienating potential allies and recruits. Thus, one interviewee writes: 'Violence [against property] . . . is legitimate, but not very helpful'. For others, violence would probably lead to state repression and hence weaken the movement. 'Violence', says an interviewee, 'would be most likely to beget more violence'.

Many balk at the attempt in the questionnaire to force a binary opposition between legitimacy and illegitimacy, and introduce instead a number of lenses through which they prefer to assess the use of violence. Several interviewees maintain that violence is *contingently* acceptable, depending on the definition of the term violence, the nature of the object or target, the agent of violence, and the availability and efficacy of other protest strategies.

Several interviewees point out that those whom they perceive as suffering under globalization are more likely to be the victims rather than the perpetrators of violence. According to these interviewees, violence gains legitimacy as a response from those subject to economic violence or state repression. 'I do not ever advocate violence', notes one interviewee, 'but if people are starving and their lives are in danger, I understand it'. This legitimacy increases when states repress movements that had adopted nonviolent strategies. In these circumstances, violence – first, against property, and sometimes against people – gains credibility as a 'last resort', defined as 'self-defense'. 'In other countries', one interviewee maintains, 'repression prevents protests. Violence can challenge the monopoly of power.'

While all interviewees dispute the notion that this strategy now makes practical sense in the US, some accept that it could have a place in other situations. One interviewee highlights the contingent view of violence: 'Pacifism is generally a privilege; we have that option here, but it is not always an option for all'.

For many, the answer turns on definitional issues. Some interviewees claim that it is essential to interrogate the term and rescue meanings deemed illegitimate by dominant groups: 'The police now define violence as sitting peacefully in the street'. Most commonly, 'property destruction' is considered to be nonviolent, as opposed to violence against persons, though many judge it unwise. These interviewees argue that through dramatic incidents against symbols of corporate power, or through boycotts and other tactics that might hurt a corporation, destruction of property is necessary as a way to check power. Similarly, many endorse 'civil disobedience' as a legitimate tactic, and would exclude it from the definition of violence, even if this disobedience might result in the destruction of property or the loss of life.

Toward a new common sense

So what is the knowledge added by this case study of *latent* and potentially emergent counterideology? The survey data show the extent to which the template of mainstream media representations is accurate. Yes, there is a strong correlation between our evidence and the mass-mediated images of globalization protesters as mostly young, highly educated, and middle class.[11] However, the media's sketch suppresses the subtle but critical distinctions noted above concerning age, minority-group participation, occupation, and income levels. The depiction of putative discrepancies among the protesters' priorities is certainly correct in that the activists hold mixed views, as with their attitudes about the role of international organizations in the globalization matrix. It is wrong though to render the protesters as rejectionists. Although core institutions such as the WTO, World Bank, and the IMF are seen as problematic, the protesters still embrace the gains of globalization, such as technological advances and greater opportunities for the mobility of peoples.

Unlike the portrait of the protesters painted by the media, in actuality the activists advance a moral critique and express discomfort with a violent strategy. Although a minority of protesters believes that the legitimacy of violence is contingent, they do not advocate violence in an unproblematic or total way. The matter of incoherence in the picture presented by the media is a question of interconnections among beliefs, attitudes, goals, and strategies. In general, elements in the protesters' broad values, their criticism of globalizing structures, and their assessment of the impact of core institutions as instruments of globalization are widely shared among the agents. These bundles are not just random collections; while not wholly coherent, there is a loose fit among the properties in a conceptual scheme.

Nevertheless, a detailed and discernible agenda is not to be found in the protesters' views. The differences identified by other analysts over goals, strategies, and tactics are certainly present in the responses of these protesters. Is this a strength or a weakness of the global justice movement? On the one hand, one might look for coalescence as a sign of strength; on the other, it may be argued that civil society flourishes with diversity and when it fosters a swarm of ideas.

To underline a main point, the interviewees' perspectives show considerable complexity and reflection, features rarely included in mass-mediated representations of the global justice movement. Again, the protesters' views do not indicate a complete rejection – 'antiglobalization' – but a selective rejection of aspects of globalization, especially neoliberal policies and the institutions that seek to universalize them.

Surprisingly, however, in answers to open-ended questions meant to compensate for any gaps in the survey instrument, little attention is given to employment growth and unemployment, or issues that are often linked to them: trade and protectionism, themes that later become more salient. Here, too, the evidence clearly indicates selectivity in priorities though not principles. There is general accord on the need for democratic accountability, redistribution of wealth and opportunities, and respect for local culture in shaping alterglobalization.

These observations provide an intensive examination of one historical moment in the trajectory of resistance to globalization. This moment is a key node in the transition from targeting primarily economic globalization to focusing on the bridge between the geoeconomic and geostrategic dimensions of globalization, which US policymakers are constructing. The April 2002 rally lies at the intersection of globalization protest and the peace movement. They add force to one another, with interlocking critiques of power structures, and could contribute to a broader synthesis of resistance. To investigate rather than speculate about these prospects, further research must undertake both historical tracking and surveys in several locales in and outside the US.

In sum, this genre of research identifies common-sense conceptions and their tacit knowledge sets, and offers an alternative to hierarchically structured disciplinary approaches. Methodologically, it emphasizes context, elicits voices from below, and engages the discourses of both hegemonic power and activists. Epistemologically, it looks beyond the assumption of formed representations among protesters to the ways in which these agents actively engage in a fluid and embryonic process of political learning to produce counterrepresentations. Pedagogically, this mode of research raises doubts about ideological represen- tations and the claims of authoritative knowledge. When students shift from the audience to actors in knowledge production, they see that globalization protests are no longer clearly defined objects of analysis but mobile and evolving spaces in the redefinition of political life. Student researchers begin to think about how common-sense meanings are produced and reproduced by powerful institutions and dominant strata. So, too, students consider the challenges mounted by critically oriented activists and intellectuals. It is well to recall that for Gramsci, critical thinking should not merely reject ingrained conceptions but become an element in people's self-reflexivity, producing a new common sense.

Moving to another context and using different methods, the analysis now looks to an additional aspect of ideology in the emergence of microresistance in Japan. The multidimensional nature of globalization and alterglobalization requires fleshing out more detail in the process of ideological formation.

7 Bringing in micro-encounters

There is a parable about a man who looks for his lost keys under the streetlights instead of where he lost them, because it is easier to look where the light is better.[1] In scholarly work too, we often search in familiar areas for what meets the eye. Thus, when it comes to resistance to globalization, one may focus on large demonstrations in major cities or public gatherings, such as the WSF, where tens of thousands of representatives of social movements from several countries have assembled, and its regional subforums.

In contrast to the aforementioned macroresistance, there is a more subtle microresistance to neoliberal globalization. As will be shown, this distinction is not a neat divide but a heuristic that facilitates examining fluid blends of forms of resistance. In developing my argument about resistance, I will draw on my research and personal experience in Japan. It is worth noting that the use of experiential knowledge, including autobiography, is deeply ingrained in critical legal studies, postcolonial studies, and some other branches of the humanistic sciences that bridge to the social sciences, as in gender studies. In this chapter, my objectives are thus to offer ideas that point to promising avenues for sustained research and, by focusing on micro-encounters, to push the current globalization debates.

The discussion starts in a conventional manner by laying out some of the main concepts that frame globalization research and defining key terms. Next is an attempt to make distinctions between different forms of resistance, using Foucault's notion of 'capillaries of power'. Then, in a departure from convention, I turn to the ways in which teams of Japanese students acted on their intuition and interrogated this line of research, generating powerful insights and identifying directions for inquiry. Taking this cue, my own research goes on to probe the questions opened by the students, and the analysis offers broad conclusions.

Perspectives on resistance to globalization

Picking up on themes in previous chapters, I have tried to build a concept of globalization that embraces a diachronic explanation, centers on spheres of control, and adopts a perspective that includes the encounters of the lower rungs of the worldwide social hierarchy, which, after all, is the majority of humankind.

To underline a key point, globalization may beget either accommodation or resistance.

Plainly, resistance is evident at head-on confrontations, such as the 1999 'Battle of Seattle' over WTO policy, protests in Washington, DC (Chapter 6) and Prague at the annual conferences of the IMF and the World Bank, demonstrations in Melbourne and New York at gatherings of the WEF, and clashes in Seoul surrounding the Asia–Europe Meeting as well as in Quebec City at the Summit of the Americas and in Genoa at the Group of Eight (G-8) Meeting. But there is an important difference between what is openly declared, such as demonstrations and strikes, and the undeclared forms of resistance. This distinction between the overt and more covert forms of resistance is not a sharp dichotomy but an entry point for understanding the many combinations of resistance in different contexts.

Inasmuch resistance to globalization is multifaceted, it can be difficult to grasp. To focus an analysis, one must pinpoint what resistance is against. Institutions, norms, rules, power systems, and/or contemporary culture? And what is resistance for?

Going further, if resistance to globalization arises in stark fashion in instances marked by a sustained economic boom, as in the US in the 1990s, then why does there seem to be a lack of such displays of resistance in the context of a major economic downturn and social disruption, which is the case in Japan? After all, in the last decade, Japan has experienced a break with the system of assured life-time employment in a single firm and, by 2002, a doubling of the official unemployment rate to a record 5.5 per cent. Job layoffs have been accompanied by a surge in immigration in a society that props up a myth of 'homogeneity', notwithstanding the presence of resident Koreans, indigenous people known as the Ainu, Okinawans whose culture differs markedly from the mainstream, and a subordinate caste of Buraku people. Income disparities grew by almost 50 per cent between 1995 and 2000, and class distinctions are mounting. But why have there not been dramatic protests in the teeth of globalization?

A key to the explanation may be found in the geographic concepts of place and space (e.g. Pile and Keith 1997; Sharp *et al.* 2000; Routledge 2000). Myriad forms of resistance to globalization are based in, but not limited to, place and span space. Hence, resistance is often dispersed and spatialized through networks, some of which may be submerged (Keck and Sikkink 1998; Melucci 1985). Or resistance to neoliberal globalization may even be formless. Moreover, just as there is resistance to hegemony, so there are hegemonic tendencies within resistance. Not only is there power to resist, but power within resistance may suppress subgroups and dissent.

Resistance, then, is about power relations. As argued, it may be read as not only a response to, but also an integral part of globalization itself. Not surprisingly, the least-understood type of resistance is the more hidden, sometimes subsurface, micro variant that emerges in myriad locales. *Microresistance* refers to countless diverse acts and beliefs that send forth ripples of doubt and questions concerning the viability and sustainability of neoliberal globalization. The micro form of resistance may be seen through a Foucaultian lens, exemplified in Japan after the bubble burst. This case is perhaps a harbinger of a succession of crises in globalization and possibly will be a pervasive feature of the twenty-first century. Finally, the importance of the distinction between micro and macroresistance to neoliberal globalization is that public debates, as represented in the media, and most scholarly discourse focus on the latter in the guise of movements, networks, and sometimes state policies, as with French subsidies for their cultural industries. Nonetheless, the micro variant is the prevailing pattern in some parts of the world and entwines with the latter in ways that have not adequately been grasped. The interplay between the micro and the macro are displayed when the former, often in the cultural and symbolic realms, provides inspiration, energy, and communication for the more visible and institutional phases of political resistance (Melucci 1996: 113–17). In practice, they meld in intricate and varied ways that Foucault's frame helps to elucidate.

Foucaultian resistance[2]

To pick up on a theme introduced in previous chapters, when compared to other theorists who explore resistance, such as Polanyi (1957), Gramsci (1971), and Scott (1990), Foucault takes a broad view of power and adopts an unusually wide perspective of politics.[3] A Foucaultian lens is distinctive in the ways in which it delimits unfamiliar bounds of resistance and the interstices of power and resistance. Known for his work on how power is used to construct the human body as a subject, Foucault did not detail a concept of resistance. Apart from a brief explicit passage in *The History of Sexuality, Volume I: An Introduction* (1990: 95–7), Foucault mentions resistance only in passing; one must extrapolate from his elusive comments in various writings (1977, 1980, 1982, 1990). Although scattered and fragmented, Foucault's thoughts on resistance are consistently tied to his concept of power.

Foucault emphasizes power relations, knowledge, and institutions in society as ways in which order is structured. For Foucault, power is not only relational, but, as discussed (Chapters 1 and 2), also fundamentally repressive and disciplining. Eschewing a meta-story about power, Foucault contends that just as power qua knowledge can induce or enforce docility, it can also authorize agents to realize themselves.

Just as power circulates in capillary forms, so too resistance operates at a capillary level. In this metaphor, the circulatory system consists of arteries and veins, which are the main conduits of blood, and the heart pumps blood through the system. However, the system largely comprises capillaries – minute vessels that enable cells to actually move blood around the body. Likewise, Foucault examines conduits of power, the sites where power flows, establishing a disciplined subject. It is in institutions that bodies are transformed into subjects. Power operates locally as a life force within social relations to maintain or, conversely, as counterpower, to attack a social order. In other words, faced with disciplinary power, the life forces of the body are the basic sources of resistance. Hence, volumes two and three of *The History of Sexuality* chronicle the struggle between the construction of the knowledge of sexuality, where disciplinary power is masked, and the body.

Is it possible to escape disciplinary power? Can non-disciplinary power relations be instituted? To what extent does Foucault offer vision of an alternative? To be sure, he provides clues to where the researcher should concentrate attention, focal points that diverge from those that appear in other prisms on resistance.

> If one wants to look for a non-disciplinary form of power, or rather, to struggle against disciplines and disciplinary power, it is not towards the ancient right of sovereignty that one should turn, but towards the possibility of a new form of right, one which must indeed be anti-disciplinarian, but at the same time liberated from the principle of sovereignty.
>
> (Foucault 1980: 108)

Thus, if disciplinary power is constituted as 'an organized multiplicity', then counterpower emanates from all these forces and 'form[s] a resistance to the power that wishes to dominate it: agitations, revolts, spontaneous organizations, coalitions – anything that may establish horizontal conjunctions' (Foucault 1977: 219). One must examine the network of power relationships to decipher diverse kinds of resistance. More specifically, a Foucaultian analysis seeks out the points of resistance to power, which may be discerned as 'the antagonism of strategies'. In Foucault's own investigations, this includes how institutions constitute and are constituted by the individual bodies that they govern.

To summarize as concisely as possible, Foucault claims that if resistance accompanies and arises from power, and if power is best understood as a flow that forms a vast multiplicity, then resistance itself is multiple – therefore, highly diffuse – and often localized. Not surprisingly, his critics have raised many objections. Is his concept of power nondiscriminating? If it is everywhere, then what does it omit? In addition, not only is Foucault silent about the strategic moment – the practicalities of actual strategies – but also he does not explain why some, yet not other, people resist (Pickett 1996: 445). He does not go far in proposing how to make resistance positive – to move toward 'a new economy of bodies and pleasures' (Dreyfus and Rabinow 1982: 207). Moreover, there is the matter of whether any activity – terrorism, for instance – can be justified in the name of resistance (Pickett 1996).

Whereas Foucault's critics raise important points, his contribution is to unmask power, which, he submits, is hidden in a social order, and to show that resistance takes place within that same order. Counterpower strips a social order of its ability to discipline a subject and make it docile. Resistance manifests at the site where power and counterpower meet head-on. If the capillaries of power are the spaces where power acts on a body to discipline it, then these are the loci where resistance emerges to contest power. Individual bodies are the sites of contestation.

It is Foucault's insight that resistance may be a flat, non-hierarchical network of power relations and that it creates a local knowledge to alter repressive power. He suggests that the body's own vital forces may establish 'biopower' – the regulation of social production and reproduction from its interior. In addition, Foucault offers a knowledge of resistance – but certainly not a programmatic guide – and a call for myriad strategies, including alternative knowledge, an emphasis on subjectivity, and the vital forces of the body as a site of struggle, all points that may be discerned in Japan's experience with globalization.

Foucault's resonance with resistance in Japan

In 2000, I taught an undergraduate course on 'Globalization' for mostly third-year students at Ritsumeikan University in Kyoto. One of their assignments, given at the initial class session, was to self-organize into research teams of four or five students each and to investigate a concrete issue on which resistance to globalization manifests in Japan. At first, one or two students *resisted* – ever so politely, of course – the task, objecting that Japan does not resist globalization. Just look at the embrace of the artifacts of global culture and the life-ways of the younger generation, as evidenced in the trendy sections of Kyoto and, more so, in Tokyo.

Not only has Japan been free of mass demonstrations against globalization, but also, at this writing, according to activists and government officials whom I interviewed, large-scale protests are not being planned. This apparent lack of openly declared resistance to globalization is puzzling given that the Japanese economy's steep decline since 1991 has been accompanied by the buying up of many of its financial institutions and other assets by foreign capital, the breakdown of a variety of once protectionist barriers, and increasing social dislocation of various sorts said to be unavoidable in the face of stiff global competition.

A part of the explanation may be that thanks to globalization, aspects of Japanese culture have become export products. Among them, notwithstanding the colonial legacy, Japanese popular entertainment, particularly music, is sought by youth in Korea and other Asian countries. A distinctive animation style embodied in 'manga' (large comic books for adults as well as children), cartoons and other films – many of which emphasize the postmodern themes of dissolving identities and collapsing institutions – has brought profit and influence. In this respect, Japan has both gained from global industries and, to a small extent, challenged Hollywood's hegemony.

Nonetheless, that there is not more manifest resistance to globalization is also perplexing when one recalls the country's long history of resistance. Indeed, the entire Japanese population was not passive or compliant during its 15-year war in Asia and Pacific (1931 to 1945). As demonstrated in the Kyoto Museum for World Peace, which brutally tells the story of militarism, Japanese writers, artists, and filmmakers mounted sharp resistance to colonialism and war. After 1945, many Japanese engaged in open resistance campaigns – highly politicized labor movements up to the 1960s, locally and later transnationally active environmental movements since the late 1960s, determined student movements (which coincided with the activities of their counterparts in France and the US) until the early 1970s, and nationwide anti-nuclear peace movements encompassing, among others, workers, students, and women throughout the postwar period (Sakamoto

2001). This resistance, however, was not waged against globalization per se. But why in a country with a living memory of rectifying grievances, is resistance to globalization muted?

Mindful of Japan's history, I encouraged my students to think more about the meaning of resistance, to take a closer look at the Japanese experience, and in conjunction with the assigned reading, to carry out careful empirical research on a specific topic. At the same time, I sought to avoid entrapping the students in a theoretical system in which the fundamental template had already been decided. In view of the epistemic debates over 'narrative entrapments' (Shotter 1993: 26–31; Chapter 4 in this book), there were efforts to allow students to escape from a predetermined theoretical standpoint. Even so, students themselves are the products of educational systems and other institutions of power.

That said, I do not know exactly when or how each research team chose its topic, but have no doubt that intuition played a part. Intuition, a means of discovery of knowledge scrutinized by Descartes and other philosophers, is used here to mean an intellectual faculty for grasping propositions about the world around the investigator. Some observers believe that this faculty is innate or a priori. Reflecting on this route to knowledge, Weber gave credence to 'the intuitive flashes of imagination as hypotheses which are then "verified" ' (1949: 176).

Reflecting students' imaginations, three of six papers focused on matters that pertain to the body, understood as sites of power.[4] The class did not read Foucault's works. I did not mention them, and as far as I can tell, they were unfamiliar to the students. It is apparent that *intuitively*, half the students found their own route to the destination at which Foucaultian theory arrives, while also pushing and grounding the theory in a place-based, but not place-limited, manner.

In a fascinating paper titled 'Globalization's Effects on Japanese Women and Their Reactions' (Ikeda, Lopez Rello, and Lundh 2000), students interviewed and distributed a questionnaire to prostitutes, hostesses, and ethnic Korean and Japanese feminists. The interviews and survey tapped attitudes on global flows, such as the transnational sex industry, that directly affect women. A Japanese professor introduced the research team to an activist whose work with the transnational NGO End Child Prostitution in Asian Tourism centers on networks that operate across borders, as evident in Osaka Prefecture. The students found that child prostitutes profess to be proud that they are feeding their families, and that in some cases, such as Meiji-era Japan as well as in parts of contemporary Southeast Asia, national development strategies have promoted prostitution. The sex industry today, the students argued, 'is a part of the larger problem of how to moderate the sometimes cruel process of the [sic] globalization'. The research team concluded on an optimistic note, holding that heightened market integration has the potential to advance women's interests and human rights, but there is a need to adapt the Japanese economy, which 'is starting to change if not crumble', to globalization.

Two other groups of students chose topics pertaining to food, also a fundamental matter of vital bodily forces, as dramatized in the tiny town of Millau,

France, where, in 1999, a sheep farmer, José Bové, demolished a McDonald's restaurant. In the view of the protesters, McDonald's symbolizes the smallholder's lack of freedom to manage the land, a world-market system of agriculture that promotes genetically altered crops, and WTO and EU trade policies concerning food, which is at the core of French culture. Bové's account – a resistant text – quickly became a best seller in France (Bové and Dufour 2000).[5]

In recent decades, the marketplace for food has of course changed substantially, with national and then global products supplanting local goods, altering price structures and consumption patterns, being integrated into a system of worldwide trade, and fundamentally affecting health. With a premonition about this, the student research teams prepared papers on 'The Resistance to Genetically Modified Foods in Japan' and 'WTO and Farming Product (Rice)'. The former paper (Arai, Inoue, Otsuki, Takayanagi, and Yamagishi 2000) shows that despite the Japanese government's support for the biotechnology industry's efforts to redesign plants using genes from other organisms, including different species, certain Japanese food companies felt obliged to address public concerns through either official pronouncements or altered policies on genetically modified products. For example, in 1997, Taishi Food Industry stated that 'we never use GM [genetically modified] crops as raw materials'. Similarly, in 1999, Kikkoman, the largest soy sauce company in Japan, changed the soybeans in its 'marudaizu' series and labeled its non-genetically modified products. The pressure came not from large-scale public demonstrations, but by expressions of concerns shared by consumers, especially the Consumers Union of Japan, and dairy farmers. Not stridently voiced, but easily elicited in interviews, the apprehension centers on uncertainty over safety, the ethical question of tampering with nature, and media coverage and advertisements regarding genetically modified foods.

Similarly, the other research paper (Kontani, Kawada, and Uemura 2000) details a quiet form of resistance, in this case by Japanese farmers and consumers. Not surprisingly, Japanese rice growers are against liberalization because they do not want to face stiff international competition. Also, opening to the global market is perceived as a threat to their identity, connections to nature, and cultural and spiritual heritage, of which rice is a principal part. Competition from overseas and mechanized technology portend the decomposition of family farming, as well as the life-ways and values attendant to it. For many Japanese consumers, the taste of foreign rice is unappealing. (Bové employed the term 'la malbouffe' – for junk food, including the fare at McDonald's, imported from the US and elsewhere.) Moreover, the pesticides applied in countries with little regulation present health risks. At bottom, the issues concerning governmental policy and the WTO's promotion of liberalization are matters of cultural dignity, food security, and environmental protection.

Taken together, the students' incisive research on these themes identifies a key and untheorized pattern:[6] Strikingly, although Japan has not experienced conspicuous confrontations over globalization, there is substantial and highly varied resistance to it. The resistance meshes several distinct forms, some of them different from the Western varieties, which, it is worth emphasizing, are themselves diverse. As such, the students have provided important pointers for empirical research, which I followed.

Japanese expressions of resistance after the bubble

Clearly, at the dawn of the twenty-first century, the main discourses in Japan concern political and economic nationalism. There is a revival of nationalism – some even say 'emperorism' – and much public debate focuses on related issues such as revising both Article 9 of the Constitution (barring rearmament) and historical accounts that present Japan as an aggressor nation in World War II. When 'chopping heads' (a Japanese expression for job dismissals) takes place, corporations try to legitimate their action by convincing displaced employees that the citizenry should be proud of economic restructuring and that they are helping to strengthen the economy. Yet a large element of the population remains disgruntled with the Japanese economy and a political system built on factionalism and bureaucracy, which embodies remnants of feudalism.

Although this self-evident dissatisfaction does not necessarily take globalization as its referent, there are indeed individuals and groups that display anger at globalization. Sex, gender, and food are palpable issues with transnational dimensions. Japanese women certainly express concern about national problems, such as sexual violence and its historical legacy extending to other countries: the state's failure to make recompense to the 'comfort women', sexual slaves during World War II. In league with feminists and peace activists in other countries, NGOs, such as the Violence against Women and War Network, Japan – known as VAWWNET-JAPAN – organized the 2000 Women's International War Crimes Tribunal on Japan's Military Sexual Slavery: a public hearing with prominent international judges and representatives of victimized countries (China, Taiwan, the Philippines, and South and North Korea) as participants, putting the Government of Japan on trial for its crimes against women during World War II.[7]

There have been efforts to fasten the transborder problems of gender, e.g. the role of migrant women in Asia's growing sex industry – to resistance to regionalism and globalization. This concern is central to the agenda of the People's Plan for the Twenty-First Century (PP21), established by various networks and NGOs in Asia in 1989, their goal being transformative and participatory democracy. During the 1990s, there were numerous attempts to breathe life into the idea of transborder democracy, including conferences, workshops, electronic communication, and the establishment of subnetworks in South Asia and elsewhere. By the turn of the century, however, the PP21 came on hard times, and now shows signs of decline. Its secretariat in Hong Kong has encountered difficulties in coordination, and the PP21 process has operated as an NGO but not primarily at the grassrooots. Nonetheless, from another angle, one might say that many people came to share the PP21 *idea*. While not unique to this group, concerns about gender and democracy require transborder coalitions for realization (Inoue 2000; Muto 2000; PP21 2000).

Likewise, women have been active and prominent in the leadership of the drive for food security and respect for ecological balance. This has involved asserting social control over techniques of production and redirecting consumption. A pertinent case is the Negros alternative, the significance of which ramifies well beyond the specific instance.

In response to a precipitous drop in world sugar prices and the closing down of plantations on the island of Negros in the Philippines, the Japan Committee for Negros Campaign (JCNC) was launched in 1986. At the same time, nationwide, the Philippine resistance drove President Ferdinand Marcos from office, and large numbers of farm workers occupied haciendas and claimed land titles. A group of Negros farmers and the JCNC, supported by consumer co-ops in Japan, addressed the problems of both working conditions and the consumers' desire for organic products as a substitute for chemically laden foods in Japanese supermarkets. Together, they decided on the Balangon banana as suitable for Japanese tastes. This food crop was not part of the producers' daily diet and would not displace the local market. It has assumed symbolic meaning and has served as a catalyst in the search for an alternative to the neoliberal model of a disembedded market. The Balangon banana – portrayed in advertisements as small, sweet, and organic, unlike the large, standard and bright yellow, chemically treated variety grown by low-wage workers – became an icon of an alternative way of organizing production and consumption. Priced at two to three times what supermarkets charge, the Balangon product represents a reverse transfer of value, one from the North to the South. Notwithstanding the markup, a large part of which is deposited in the Negros fund for self-reliant agriculture, demand for this banana exceeds supply. Despite certain setbacks, including typhoons, disease afflicting the plants, armed violence prompted by guerrillas, and errors in management, the growers – beneficiaries of the fund – have experienced increases in average household income (from 500–800 pesos to 1500–2000 pesos per month during the early 1990s), improvements in their diet and housing, and greater availability of health care and schools (Hotta 2000; Hotta forthcoming).

At a Tokyo meeting of representatives of the two sides, I was struck by their class membership – small farmers from Negros, Japanese workers (many of them in the service sector), and mostly the lower reaches of the middle class. Together, these groups have sought to resist not the market economy but market society. They have attempted to establish control over a circuit of production and consumption without mediation by the state. This project includes reciprocal visits between the two communities so that social and political relations, based on trust and mutual support, are generalized beyond trade. The strategy is a way to reconcile the principles of self-determination and autonomy on the one hand, and initiatives that supersede the principle of territoriality, enshrined as a cornerstone of sovereignty, on the other.

Nonetheless, on balance, the impact of the Negros initiative is limited. Only 2,000 families on Negros Island are supported by this banana trade; it serves no more than 65,000 consumers in Japan, thus providing a small fraction of the country's total imports of bananas. Yet with 12 million members connected to 'bioregional' producers outside the conventional food chain, in some cases threatening the viability of supermarkets, the consumer co-ops have grown exponentially; organic production in Japan, much of it local, rose from around zero to 14 per cent of all food output by 1994 (Hotta forthcoming). Not only has Alter Trade Japan formed a partnership with Alter Trade Philippines, but also the former has launched similar projects for importing shrimp from Indonesia (like the Philippines, a country that suffered at the hands of Japanese militarism) and Kilimanjaro coffee from Tanzania (Hotta 2000). Then, too, in resisting 'free trade', fair trade groups in the North, including Alter Trade Japan, have established contact with other Northern-based alternative trading organizations as well as groups in the South, and set up the International Federation of Alternative Trade, which extends beyond agriculture to various sectors such as the handicraft industry. In short, the lessons of the Negros alternative are far-reaching. The potential for other initiatives is vast in terms of generalizing this prototype, and the overall experience, while not immune from serious problems, is emblematic of an evolving ethic of resistance that blends the macro and micro variants.

Cosmodrama

The leadership of Alter Trade Japan was trained in drama and emerged from the theater, not the academy, to resist the policy framework of neoliberal globalization. But its productions are not being seen on the world stage. Notice today is paid mainly to the drama performed in certain global cities, with the key actors cast as street warriors leading the charge against both international institutions and, on another stage, the billing accorded the power holders by their enthusiasts (Friedman 1999; Ohmae 1999; Micklethwait and Wooldridge 2000), although there are also critical – one might say resistant – reviews (Gills 2000; Klein 1999; Starr 2000).

Today, the 'Battle of Seattle' has become a galvanizing metaphor for macro-resistance, which signals a new dynamic in globalization: a political intervention by a coalition of heterogeneous citizens' groups in a globalizing economy. These groups came from many different locales, including Japan, to Seattle and the other cities where mass protests were mounted. But what about the venues where these demonstrations – which bridge left and right, and bring together groups that want a seat at the table with those who want to destroy it – have not occurred?

In answer, the focus on macroresistance draws attention to powerful organizations, apparent processes, and important venues like the WEF. However, it risks neglecting the micro and silencing the crucial question of the interplay of the micro and the macro.

As discussed, a Foucaultian framework shifts observation to the micro level, including underrepresented acts of resistance. Picking up on Foucault's point that by forming disciplined individuals – arguably, as with the constitution of power in Japan, including in the Gramscian realm of the institutions of civil society – hegemonic power may hinder the open display of resistance, although anger is expressed in more circumspect ways. Certainly, institutions such as the

Japanese family, schools, and religion have served as disciplinary forces in a society that values conformity. (As one of my students in Kyoto demurred when I called for critical evaluation of assigned readings, 'We are taught to be ordinary'.)

This line of argument may be used to explain the general course of Japanese history until 1945. However, in the postwar period, as a critical response to the past, labor, environmental, student, and anti-nuclear peace movements, while diverse, all have served to make the people more autonomous, less tied to the state, despite its paternalism, without which democracy, first imposed during the US occupation, could not have taken root in Japan (Sakamoto 2001; Nakatani n.d.).

> The anti-nuclear peace movements were simultaneously a demilitarization movement and a democratization movement because they aimed at empowering the people to exercise control over the foreign policy making – the crucial condition in the absence of which the Japanese people had become both the perpetrators and victims of war under militarism.
>
> (Sakamoto 2001)

At present, these popular movements appear to be quiescent, giving the appearance of tranquility, especially when order is maintained. But one must dig beneath the surface, for as Braudel aptly put it: '[D]o not believe that only the actors which make the most noise are the most authentic – there are other, quieter ones too' (1980: 38). In Japan, state power is in crisis, especially in terms of legitimacy; there is declining public confidence in the ruling Liberal Democratic Party and the state bureaucracy. Is the tranquility then only an appearance, not a subsurface phenomenon, in a context in which the agents of discipline, including the family and the school system, are rapidly disintegrating? This anomie is particularly marked among youth, and also, as Sakamoto (2001) has pointed out, is caught up in struggles over identity, including resurgent nationalism on the one hand and searches for transnational solidarity on the other.

Still, it would be a grave error to lose sight of the fact that globalization has brought major benefits to Japan. Transnational competition has helped to lower the prices of many consumer goods, and neoliberalism has contributed to the downsizing of the state bureaucracy, a popular measure given the many scandals associated with it, some of them involving 'legal' corruption in the interlacing of political and corporate power structures.

Nevertheless, the framework advanced here sensitizes one to the less-evident resistance against the dark side of globalization. Perhaps it provides a different way of thinking about resistance to globalization, blurring some of the heretofore resilient categories ingrained in the social sciences. In addition, without erring by purporting to understand the whole in terms of its parts, this framework avoids the pitfalls of both economism and structuralism, which banish agents and fail to allow them to write their own history. This frame by no means entails turning a blind eye to regressive resistances, an inflation of the microcosm, or a postmodern celebration of diversity. Rather, it shows that a large part of resistance to globalization is scattered and differentiated, private and intimate, personal as well as public. It shows that this resistance is local and yet may be parallel to, or blended with, responses in other parts of the world. It shows that a key aspect of the cosmodrama may not be high drama, as in the theater of Seattle, but the scenes enacted in ways of life, many of them more improvised than rehearsed.

My point is that if one extends a Foucaultian perspective, as in Japan after the bubble, clearly resistance to globalization is, in good measure, remarkably micro, a pattern freighted with macro significance. If so, the next step is to grasp the manifold ways in which microresistance and macroresistance are mediated. This is a matter of whether agents are empowered to, or disempowered from, compressing the time and space between these structures.

By focusing on multiple forms of cross-cutting resistances, we can read power in a more dispersed and less systemic fashion. Yet one pattern stands out: all the cases brought to light by both the students and my own research are of microresistance already linked in one way or another to macro projects or even corporate power. Alter Trade, for example, is both an agent of resistance and a registered corporation that complies with the law and pays taxes to the state. Perhaps even more than Foucault indicated, there is ambiguity within the ambiguity of biopower. Indeed, biopower can be wielded by the weak as well as the strong. Fundamentally, a priority in research is to go beyond my study of cultural and institutional mediation in Japan and uncover the whole series of mediations among resistances, which are central to the historical transformation known as globalization. The transformative possibilities include opening space for different forms of alterglobalization.

Part IV

Transformative possibilities

8 Alterglobalization

As the indomitable Margaret Thatcher once remarked about neoliberal global-ization, 'There is no alternative'.[1] Known as TINA, this slogan means that globalization in its present form is here to stay. Was she right?

Not at all. To understand why not, let's look beyond immediate events, however compelling they may be, and adopt Braudel's *longue durée* perspective. The focus is on a long horizon that extends to the future of globalization – alternatives to its current constitution.

Indeed, globalization can be politically disempowering if one regards it as a juggernaut, i.e. a totalizing force governing history. Two factors have tended to subordinate the politics of globalization. First, there is the rush to implement neoliberal policies that promote market integration. Second, there is a preoccu-pation with market growth rather than balanced development or equity. What, then, are the possibilities for recapturing politics and the prospects for making it work for the world's majority?

In answering this question, I want to argue that globalization has opened spaces, expanding the boundaries associated with political life. Of course, one cannot predict the future from a set of structural tendencies. But one can gauge the balance of constraints and possibilities. History is fundamentally propelled by human will, albeit subject to evolving global forces; it is an open-ended process. If globalization was made by humankind, then it can be unmade or remade by political agency. As with slavery, feudalism, and mercantile capitalism, there is no reason to believe that neoliberal globalization is eternal.

Neoliberal globalization as utopia

Sponsors of globalization seek to create a global market in which the peoples of the world increasingly relate to each other only as individuals. Putting it baldly, Margaret Thatcher declared, 'There is no such thing as society, only individual men and women and their families'. If so, neoliberalism thus under-mines society, making it ancillary to the market. From this perspective, neoliberal globalization is an attempt to achieve the utopia of freeing the market from social and political control. It is a utopia in the sense that this condition has never existed.

Not only is the utopia of a free market comprised of individual actors ahistorical, but also, in Polanyi's memorable phrase, '*Laissez-faire* was planned; planning was not' (Polanyi 1957: 141). In an earlier century, concerted action by a liberal state in Great Britain spawned a supposedly self-regulating economy, yet the pressure for ensuing anti-*laissez-faire* legislation beginning in 1860 started in a spontaneous manner and picked up gradually. Notwithstanding a variety of such enactments, the opening of the so-called free market fomented an 'economic earthquake': a trajectory from social control over the market to a disembedding of market activities. The market gained autonomy, diminishing society relative to market power; in turn, this realignment provoked a protectionist countermovement from social forces, particularly the English working class (see Chapter 2 above). In his challenge to the myth of a self-running market, Polanyi not only unmasked economic liberalism by providing an account of the dystopia of market society, but also pointed to the need to *re-embed* market forces in society. What must be explicated, however, are the meaning of and strategies for this re-embedding – in the contemporary era, alterglobalization.

Globalization in flux

Globalization calls into question the ability of the existing interstate system to cope with certain fundamental transnational problems. After all, the Westphalian model of states is a relic of the seventeenth century, established in the West and grafted on to other parts of the world. Strains on this system include the properties of new technologies – interconnectivity and lightning speed – as well as massive concentrations of private economic power that dwarf the resources of many national units and challenge state sovereignty.

Of course, the state does not remain idle. Those who hold the reins of power try to adjust by accommodating global flows and turning them to national and local advantage. Not all states suffer to the same extent from power deflation. So, too, it would be a mistake to portray global processes and the state as locked into a zero-sum relationship. With globalization, some elements within the state gain power while others lose. Among the winners are the economic portfolios and administrative agencies dealing with the external realm. Meanwhile, the offices charged with responsibility for social policy are reduced in scope (Cox, R.W. 1987: 228–9). Nevertheless, to varying degrees, all states, including the US, even with its unilateral and militarized policies, are losing autonomy in the emerging multilevel system. Quite clearly, states operate in a rapidly changing context. The interstate system is durable, but despite its persistence, when are states free to act independently of market constraints? While the state seeks to harness the market, market power also disciplines the state, such as with IMF conditionalities and currency speculation.

Against this backdrop, the state is reconstituting itself, attempting to be proactive in order to steer globalizing processes. However, the capacities of various states to tame these processes differ markedly. The general pattern is the reduction of regulatory activity and the lowering of barriers, although the response to September 11 includes an attempt to tighten border controls and build military security. The reconfiguring of the state means that it is becoming more of a facilitator of globalizing activities insofar as they are localized within the domain of a sovereign entity (Cox, R.W. 1987: 253–65; and for an opposing point of view, see Weiss 1998).

To aggregate their power, states have established a highly institutionalized system. Not only has there been a proliferation of international organizations in recent decades, but also, when faced with new problems of globalization such as transnational cybercrime, the holders of state power seek a higher level of institutionalization in some spheres and more effective coordination in the interstate system. Hence, there are many rounds of summitry in forums such as the G-8 for the most powerful countries, and the Group of 15, expanded to 22 for some meetings, in the developing world. Another formula, increasingly evident, is informal attempts at policy coordination, e.g. in the WEF. An additional informal mode of governance is the Trilateral Commission, which consists of corporate, political, and intellectual leaders from the advanced capitalist countries. In addition, privatized forms of governance are becoming more prominent. The structural power wielded by legal and financial services firms (Sassen 1996) and credit-rating agencies, such as Moody's and Standard & Poors, is based on evaluations of national economies that enable borrowers to raise money, or prevent them from doing so, and influences the terms of loans (Sinclair 1994a, 1994b). This power can make or break certain developing economies.

The nub of the problem is that the interstate system relies on national institutional forms at a level that does not correspond to an increasing portion of the world's political and economic activities. This incongruity between the cage of the nation-state and actual global flows is an invitation to use more fully the political imagination. Globalization, at bottom, involves a quest for an appropriate temporal and spatial scale for governance (Jessop 1997). But in this quest, what are the alternatives? The alternatives, I believe, are constituted not by well-meaning proposals that wish away the problems of power and conflict of interests, but by countervailing power, which, as we have seen, today means a multiplicity of resistances to neoliberal globalization and points to alterglobalization.

Resistances

Although Margaret Thatcher's argument about TINA is correct insofar as neoliberalism is predominant and may not have run its course, there are grounds for questioning the triumphalism reflected in her contention. This point is evident in South Africa, where, as the poet Dennis Brutus put it, there is a struggle between TINA and THEMBA, which in the Zulu language, stands for 'There must be an alternative', or, in short, 'hope' (Bond 1995: 3, 7). To be sure, it is important to ask whether the neoliberal way of ordering the world will stay or wane. Like prior forms of capitalism, neoliberalism has a history, and histories have their beginnings and ends. Certainly, neoliberalism will not simply peter out of its own accord. Rather, faced with myriad discontents and counterpressure, neoliberalism

Conclusion

is being challenged by various forces that are incipient, but, arguably, mounting. Especially noteworthy is the drive, rapidly gaining momentum, toward *reregulation*, particularly apparent in Latin America and evident elsewhere as well. Among the reasons for this trend were ways in which the 1997–8 Asian economic crisis deeply affected other regions and the buildup of social problems linked to neoliberal policies.

In different contexts, resistance has emerged not only in the public sphere, but as the previous chapter shows, also in the private, more personal, and even intimate realm. To underscore the main argument in Chapter 7, the resistance is not necessarily loudly voiced by the state or civil society; it may be quietly expressed in the life-ways of individuals and may be uncongealed. This micro-resistance is not merely against an imposing structure but may contain positive and affirmative elements. Indeed, the distinctive features of the Japanese case suggest that there are several forms of alterglobalization and no single best worldwide strategy for making globalization work. It would be facile to search for a universal solution to a vast range of complex problems that manifest differently in various locales with distinctive histories, cultures, and resource endowments. There is no realizable alternative of a kind that is good for all times and places. But are there prototypes, patterns from which alternatives for remaking globalization can be derived?

Scenarios for alterglobalization

The evidence points to a range of efforts to imagine alternatives and convert them into practice. They fall into three basic groups. The first involves modifications in neoliberal globalization without challenging its underlying structures, while the second and third call for the destruction of this paradigm, entailing an attack on the ideas and type of policies that form the bedrock of neoliberalsim.

The first group takes as axiomatic the proposition that within the globalization matrix itself there are real choices. Notwithstanding structural constraints, especially the rise of hypercompetition and the residual impact of the bygone 'Washington consensus', the choice is essentially a political one. It is held that the market can benefit society while to some extent being kept at bay by innovative state policies.

In the vortex of enormous pressure to globalize more, France exemplifies a resistant state, one that maintains much regulation, generous welfare provisions (in schooling, health care, vacations, retirement, and unemployment entitlements), and a large government-run infrastructure, such as its reliable subways and rail networks. Its critics point to a high unemployment rate far exceeding that of the US; a mounting budget deficit; frequent strikes and demonstrations impeding daily life, if not rendering it chaotic; and labyrinthine labor legislation, banking codes, and an educational system that discourages innovation. Faced with the Anglo-American model of neoliberalism, and urged to adopt 'the American solution', President Jacques Chirac responded that his country has a global sense of itself and will fight to maintain a way of life: 'France', he said, 'intends to remain France' (as quoted in Truehart 1997). In the face of unpopular changes to meet intensifying global economic pressures, a nationalist backlash is thus emerging not only from the disadvantaged segments of society but also from some states themselves. France's resistance, of course, is atypical, far different from the courtesan role played by some states in serving interests embodied in neoliberal globalization.

There are several modes of adaptation to globalization and no dearth of proposals for institutional reform. In the domestic arena, important adjustments in administrative agencies and legal procedures – say, in the field of immigration – can alleviate some of the problems brought by globalization. In the realm of finance, proposed national reforms include tougher bank standards, curbs on hedge funds, an 'exit tax', which would penalize investors for quickly withdrawing their money from a country, and other forms of reregulation. Crucially, social policy may blunt the sharp edges of the market, especially the global trend toward increased income inequality (Teeple 1995). Advocates of safety nets and social clauses are pushing in this direction, but skeptics contend that they may serve as public relations devices deflecting attention from more fundamental issues. To be sure, there is debate about the proper role of the state in the provision of public goods: specifically, in eliminating absolute poverty, dispensing piped water as well as electricity and modern sanitation for all citizens, protecting the environment, supporting the family as a unit, alleviating congested cities, curbing escalating crime, stopping corruption and cronyism, and promoting the equality of women and the rights of children. If there is a political will for such measures, then the appropriate scale for these interventions may be transnational as well.

Globally, calls for reform include some of the basic conditions on which the IMF insists, notably transparency and greater accountability by government, aspects of structural adjustment that even the fund's critics find laudable. (However, some of them add that the IMF practices double standards by maintaining secrecy in its operations and that the fund should take its own prescription.) In practice, adopting the formula of transparency and accountability requires that regimes confront the political economy of domination, often the very basis of their political support. Hence, many leaders, as was the case in Suharto's Indonesia, have found themselves in the dilemma of desperately needing foreign capital and yet reluctant or unwilling to commit political suicide by dismantling the structures of dominance that sustain the state.

Another proposal for international reform is the Tobin tax, which would place a small charge on cross-border capital flows in order to discourage the rapid transfers by speculators that upset vulnerable economies. Suggestions also include the creation of an 'early warning system', alerting the world to approaching economic trends, a global central bank, and semifixed exchange rates among leading currencies. There can be little doubt about the need for institutional reform, but for the foreseeable future, it is difficult to conceive of heads of state galvanized to agree on and implement a new architecture for global governance, let alone wield the wherewithal to rein in corporate power, which, after all, is transnationally constituted and thus largely escapes the jurisdiction of sovereign entities. More fundamentally, these alternatives cannot work if they fail to come to grips with the power relations imbued in globalization. At bottom, a really 'new international financial architecture' would entail, or require, a new political architecture.

The second order of alternatives calls for structural change, and seeks to rewrite the script of neoliberal globalization. On the right of the political spectrum, activists and intellectuals have sought to reassert identities based on membership in religious, racial, ethnic, or linguistic communities subject to globalizing forces, often personified by the immigrant, a representation of the Other. Movements based in religion have reacted sharply to the convulsive processes of globalization, in what is partly a recognition of the ways in which globalizing tendencies are undermining the values of community and ripping the social fabric. Inasmuch as neoliberal globalization facilitates cross-boundary flows, challenges national culture, and tolerates immigration, right-wing movements, especially in Europe and the US, have opposed major elements in this structure, though not market society per se. Not only have xenophobic groups invoked a sense of nativism, but also there has been opposition to regional schemes, such as NAFTA and the attempt to expand it beyond Mexico into Chile and throughout South America, on the grounds that they weaken sovereignty and are a precursor to world government. The right's political project embraces the principle of sovereignty and would build a fortress around territorially bound notions of the state, thereby implicitly calling for the downfall of globalization.

In the search for alternatives, there is a third, also structural, yet even more embryonic project that similarly poses the question, is globalization indefinitely sustainable? The torchbearers of this effort represent a broad constellation of social forces, generally the victims of globalization, elements in civil society, some politicians, and organic intellectuals. They do not advocate a status quo ante; there is no going back to preglobalization conditions, and the Keynesian welfare state of bygone decades is not the solution either. Unlike the right, this group would promote the relaxation of sovereignty in favor of identities at other levels, which would involve redrawing the boundaries of political economy. This project affirms the importance of engaging yet localizing the global, and of bottom–up processes. If anything, this latter project entails a greater diffusion of power. It includes new venues for experimentation and re-inventing the relations among the market, state, and society. It is an effort to redefine politics, to expand the space for nonstate politics. It calls for participatory democratic control of market forces, which ultimately is a matter of political agency. It is also a matter of asserting, relative to globalizing forces, greater *autonomy* – a political and moral concept used by ancient Greek writers, in a somewhat different sense by social contract theorists, and in Kantian ethics.

The core of autonomy is self-determination – a tenet that resonates with contemporary liberalism, as illustrated by aspects of John Rawls's theory of justice (1993). The principle of autonomy implies that agents have the capacity for critical reflection and, notwithstanding structural pressures, the right to choose among options. Exercising this right requires some control over conditions and actions. The principle of autonomy thus means political and economic self-governance by the majority, and allows for freedom and equality in pursuit of the 'common good' (Held 1995: 146–47; and on the coupling of globalization and democratic theory, Rosow 1999; Patomäki and Teivainen 2002; and Patomäki 2003). Building autonomy from below should not be confused with fencing-off and attempting to erect a fortress against the world, actions that could disable civil-society responses to globalization that in fact often gain strength from their transnational elements.

An assertion of autonomy from below eventually requires topping up: initiatives within the arena of state politics to bring about greater accountability. After all, the netherworld below the state can be a perilous place, usually marked by fragmentation and sometimes by intolerance and authoritarian forms of identity politics at odds with democratic life. In the face of the drive by neoliberalism to limit the scope of the state (both its activities and budget) and enforce market discipline, a strong state permitting broad access to power and a vibrant civil society pressing for democratic politics, as exemplified by the new environmental and feminist movements, stand to strengthen one another and possibly serve as a counterpoint to globalization from above (Walzer 1999). Although there is no reason to believe that the nation-state is everlasting, at present the state and civil society, with their many joint members, seem to need each other in the quest for *democratic globalization.*

From this standpoint, one response to neoliberal globalization is to pose the question, is it ethically sustainable? Morally and politically, is it possible to maintain a global system in which 5 per cent of the world's population receives 114 times the income of the poorest 5 per cent? In which the richest 1 per cent has the income of the poorest 57 per cent? And in which 25 million Americans take in as much income as almost 2 billion people (UNDP 2003: 39, citing Milanovic 2002: 51–92)? Is it ethically defensible to claim that this is the price paid for the gains that accompany expanding market forces? Or would it be better to attempt to reduce the cost by searching for a democratic solution, which is, above all, a normative preference? Surely this would not be a panacea; there are different versions of democratic theory, and as emphasized, normative preferences cannot be realized without countervailing power. The major points of countervailing power seem to be nonstate forces, not all of which are pro-democracy. In fact, they include terrorist networks.

Post-9/11 globalization and alterglobalization

Did the terrorist attacks on the Pentagon and World Trade Center, icons of US power and global capitalism, change globalization? Have the September 11 terrorists killed hopes for alterglobalization?

It would be a grave error to confuse the acute pain inflicted on September 11 and a chronic condition. The terrorist attacks did not demolish the durable structures of globalization. While homeland security is a top priority on the US policy agenda, basic trends marking globalization, especially global market integration and the expansion of regional processes, endure. Surely the underlying issues have not gone away.

Global terrorism and globalization are closely intertwined. Both are trans-border phenomena that challenge the territorial basis of state sovereignty. Both rely on modern technologies and worldwide financial networks. And while global terrorism feeds on marginalization, globalization spawns it.

Some of the poor and disenfranchised, especially in countries with repressive and corrupt governments, have sought to escape debilitating conditions, including unemployment rates of around 60 per cent for young males. In societies in which fatalism – as in the expression *In sha Allah*, or 'Whatever God wills' – is common-place and where *madrassas* (Muslim religious schools) have radicalized youth, it is not difficult to enlist marginalized people in suicide missions. These marginals believe that their deadly acts provide a ticket to paradise. Although their leaders are drawn from the middle classes and some of them are bankrolled by wealthy brethren, festering discontent fills a pool of on-the-spot losers in the globalization scenario, some of whom can be recruited into terrorist activities.

Global terrorists and globalizers alike propagate what they regard as universal truths. On the one side, terrorists and those who abet them use the idiom of religious values to control behavior – of women, children, and all those labeled 'nonbelievers'. On the other side, the beneficiaries of globalization also attempt to disseminate a value system – depicted in Chapters 1 and 4 as the freedom of markets, competition, efficiency, consumerism, and individualism – to promote a different vision of the way in which societies should be ordered.

These competing visions are in no sense morally equivalent, but the parallel rhetoric of the protagonists, Osama bin Laden and President George W. Bush, is striking: a *jihad*, or holy war that pits believers against 'infidels', versus a 'crusade' led by the US government, also the torchbearer of globalization, against 'evildoers'. The US has sought to use its power to define the global agenda as a war on terrorism, not a war against poverty, disease, and environmental harm.

Put in perspective, the globalization of terrorism is one in a series of setbacks for neoliberal globalization. The first setback was the defeat of the Multilateral Agreement on Investment, a treaty introduced by the US in the Organization for Economic Development and Cooperation in1995. Far-reaching in scope, its objectives were to remove barriers to foreign trade and extend capital markets. A coalition of citizens' groups pressured their governments to withdraw from the negotiations, though they could be resurrected in the WTO.

Second, the 1997–8 Asian financial crisis was not really Asian but global, for it rippled to Brazil, South Africa, Russia, and elsewhere. It was about the risks of globalization. Directing his strident rhetoric at Soros and other currency speculators, Malaysian Prime Minister Mahathir, a leader in the mainstream Islamic world, found his country – indeed the entire region and beyond – in a dilemma: notwithstanding its power relations and hierarchical structure, including the US's empire-like tendencies, no single entity really governs globalization.

Third, as discussed, the 1999 'Battle of Seattle' not only buffeted the WTO but more generally signaled resistance to economic globalization. Quite clearly, that event and subsequent street demonstrations in world cities on five continents represent rage over the underside of contemporary globalization.

Then, on September 11 the resistance perpetrated by a global network reached a crescendo that took the form of atrocities. The terrorism crisis is a globalization crisis. The root issue is the same set of heavily American values deemed loathsome by not only the terrorists but also several resistance movements (which, none-theless, do not endorse the grotesque September 11 tactics). As with the US-led invasion of Iraq in 2003 and the subsequent occupation, the response to terrorism by dominant powers is to militarize the structures of globalization.

To come to grips with the implications of September 11 and the aftermath for globalization, it is worth recalling Adlai Stevenson's admonition when US ambassador to the United Nations. He quipped that the modern technology that Americans most need is a hearing aid. What must be heard today, above all, are messages about different value systems. Yet notwithstanding Stevenson's reproach, however great the potential benefits of technology they alone will not remedy the challenges to world order. Rather, a thesis in this book is that an appreciation of the subjective dimensions of power – knowledge and ideology – can help identify how to alter a form of globalization guided by an insistence on absolute values that produce marginalization and despair.

The vortex of knowledge and ideology

Threaded through the foregoing chapters is the argument that globalization is not only about the material structure of power but also constitutes, and is constituted by, ways of interpreting and representing the world. The production of subjec-tivity involves knowing and portraying historical development. In this vortex, there is no single logic or sole structure of power. Just as there is global hegemony, so globalization is associated with an expansion of nonstate politics. This shift does not necessarily mean a loss of state power. Rather, the structural power of various states differs, and there is a restructuring of the state. In a contradictory manner, the power of some state agencies and functions is diminished while that of others is enhanced. The former tendency is especially apparent in the realm of social policy; the latter, in the military sphere, at least for some states as they respond to nonstate actors, especially transnational criminal organizations and terrorist networks.

However grave the threat, power agents must give an account of their own context and enterprise. They give impetus to what constitutes the dominant knowledge about globalization. In this sense, the power of globalization does not determine but conditions the cognitive realm. Globalization thus appears as a cognitive map constituted by clusters of knowledge. Euphemistically, it takes on the aura of 'the knowledge economy' or an 'information society'.

The global power structure may then operate as a closed system, thwarting the cognitive power to challenge its representations; or it can open to alternative knowledge and ideas – in short, alterglobalization. Just as these dynamics belie the dualism of proglobalization versus antiglobalization, there is not simply a clash between globalization and alterglobalization but rather multiple positions. Given the fluidity of myriad mediations between structures and agents, globalization and alterglobalization are not necessarily discrete choices. They are contingent and blend in complex ways.

Power and dominant knowledge rarely operate without ideological representations, which have both manifest and latent content. Hence, to justify themselves, power agents attempt to secure consent, which as Gramsci taught us, is the principal component of hegemony. Along with its subjective content, there is an element of brute force, which may be threatened or invoked in various measures. The ratio shifts according to historical conditions. After 9/11 and post-Saddam, a time of mounting micro- and macroresistance to globalization, the coercive ingredient has clearly become more pronounced. The ideological element of hegemony is in decline, yet subject to efforts to refresh and renew it.

In this context, intellectual power contests hegemony by bringing to light the corpus of common-sense knowledge, unmasking the ideology of globalization, and showing the ways in which cognitive and symbolic representations are linked to interests. This task goes beyond debunking. It is to open up transformative possibilities, insinuate them in common-sense knowledge, and possibly create new common sense.

In order to constitute new common sense about globalization, the epistemology of resistance incorporates mainstream presumptions of pregiven representations, new empirical information, and counterrepresentations. A critical epistemology institutes a double pedagogy of active learning in academe and by the authors of resistance themselves. These agents are not merely objects of analysis but the producers of a pedagogy that, while incipient and however fitful, can become a means of empowerment.

To generate new common sense, the creative mills of critical globalization studies produce alternative knowledge and powerful counterrepresentations. The method involves elements or combinations of the following: scrutinizing the language used to frame globalizing processes, revealing the institutions in which knowledge and ideology are created, locating an analysis within definite cultural contexts, listening to different voices and eliciting a multitude of common-sense assumptions, engaging embodied and lived experiences, and projecting grounded utopias. At bottom, implementation of a grounded utopia requires empowering its agents. It is the responsibility of critical intellectuals to strive to discover the ways to achieve alterglobalization so as to realize a peaceful, democratic, and equitable transformation. A civilized future requires no less.

Appendix: The survey questionnaire

Interviewer Code: _____

I am part of a group of students and professors from American University surveying resistance to globalization, and I would really appreciate the chance to get your views. The survey is for research purposes only, and we guarantee that your answers are completely anonymous. It should take about 10 minutes.

We'd first like to ask you a few questions about your background.

1   What is your gender?

Male 1
Female 2

2   How old are you?

Under 20. 1
20–24 2
25–29 3
30–34 4
35–39 5
40–49 6
Over 50 7

3   Of what country are you a citizen? _____

4   What is the highest level of education you have completed?

Some high school 1
Completed high school 2
Technical degree/certificate 3
Some college 4
Completed college degree 5
Some graduate school 6
Completed graduate degree 7
Completed PhD 8

5   Do you regard yourself as a member of a minority group?

Yes 1
No 2

6   How many languages do you speak proficiently?

One 1
Two 2
Three 3
Four or more 4

7   What is your main occupation? [pick one only]

Executive/Managerial/Administrative 1
Professional/Technical 2
Clerical/Administrative 3
Craftsman/Manual laborer 4
Student 5
Unemployed 6
Retired 7
Other 8

8   Roughly, what is your annual household income?

Less than 10,000 1
Between 10,000 and 24,999 2
Between 25,000 and 49,999 3
Between 50,000 and 100,000 4
More than 100,000 5
Don't know 9
Refuse 0

Now a few questions about your links to people around the world.

9   With how many people in other countries are you in regular contact
      through email?

Fewer than 10 1
Between 10 and 30 2
More than 30 3
Not in regular contact via email 4

10 How often do you use the Internet to network with other like-minded people?

Daily 1
Not every day, but one or more times per week 2
Not every week, but one or more times per month 3
Less than once a month 4
Never 5

11 How frequently do you travel outside your own country?

More than once a year 1
Once a year 2
Not every year, but occasionally 3
Never 4

Next we would like to ask questions about your political experience.

12 Are you involved in any of the following movements' organizations?

	Yes, as an officeholder	Yes, as an active member	Yes, as a non-active member	No	Don't know
1 Global justice	1	2	3	4	9
2 Labor	1	2	3	4	9
3 Environmental	1	2	3	4	9
4 Anti-nuclear	1	2	3	4	9
5 Women's rights	1	2	3	4	9
6 Peace	1	2	3	4	9
7 Civil rights	1	2	3	4	9
8 Gay and Lesbian rights	1	2	3	4	9
9 Other	1	2	3	4	9

13 Have you participated in any of the following global justice protest activities?

	Yes, as an organizer	Yes, as a protester	Yes, as a petitioner	Yes, followed events in the news	No
Seattle	1	2	3	4	5
Stockholm	1	2	3	4	5
Washington (April 2000)	1	2	3	4	5
Quebec City	1	2	3	4	5
Genoa	1	2	3	4	5
Washington (Sept 2001)	1	2	3	4	5
Other	1	2	3	4	5

Next, we'd like to ask some questions about today's protests.

14   How far did you travel to get here today?

Less than 50 miles 1
Between 51–100 miles 2
101 to 500 miles 3
501–1000 miles 4
More than 1000 miles 5
Don't know 9

15   How frequently have you used the following forms of the Internet to gather
      information about these protests?

	Often	Sometimes	Never	Don't know
Web sites	1	2	3	9
Chatrooms	1	2	3	9
Listservs	1	2	3	9
Emails	1	2	3	9

16   To what degree did the information you found on the Internet influence
      your desire to participate in these protests?

A lot 1
Moderately 2
Very little 3
Not at all 4
Don't know 9

17   What is the most important reason why you are here today?
      [Circle the best answer.]

      1   To abolish international financial institutions.
      2   To reform international financial institutions.
      3   To protest capitalism.
      4   To oppose current US foreign policy.
      5   Other

17a   If you selected 17.5 ('Other'), would you care to elaborate on your
      answer?

_____

18 Do you believe that on balance the following institutions have a positive or negative effect on ordinary people in the world?

	Very positive	Positive	Not much effect either way	Negative	Very negative	Don't know
1 United Nations	1	2	3	4	5	9
2 International security organizations (e.g. NATO)	1	2	3	4	5	9
3 Regional organizations (e.g. European Union)	1	2	3	4	5	9
4 Nongovernmental organizations (NGOs)	1	2	3	4	5	9
5 Multinational corporations	1	2	3	4	5	9
6 World Bank	1	2	3	4	5	9
7 World Trade Organization	1	2	3	4	5	9
8 International Monetary Fund	1	2	3	4	5	9

19 Here's a list of features associated with globalization. Do you think these are benefits or costs for ordinary people in the world?

Feature	Benefit	Cost	Don't know
1 Reducing government expenditure on health, education and social welfare	1	2	9
2 Privatization of state run enterprises	1	2	9
3 Export promotion	1	2	9
4 Altering local cultures	1	2	9
5 Technological advances	1	2	9
6 Increasing migration	1	2	9
7 Greater availability of consumer goods	1	2	9
8 Changing income distribution	1	2	9

20 Does globalization affect you personally?

Yes 1
No 2
Don't know 9

20a If you answered 'Yes' to question 20, on balance how does globalization affect the quality of your life?

Globalization enhances my quality of life 1
Globalization diminishes my quality of life 2
Don't know 9

21   What is your response to the following statement?

'Violence is a legitimate strategy in protesting globalization.'

Agree strongly 1
Agree somewhat 2
Neither agree nor disagree 3
Disagree somewhat 4
Disagree strongly 5
Don't know 9
Refuse 0

21a Would you care to elaborate on your answer?

_____

22   Do you have any additional reflections?

_____

Thank you very much for your time and cooperation.

Notes

Preface

1 Elsewhere (Gill and Mittelman 1997), we have discussed many of these theoretical innovations, and I will not cover the same ground in this book. A discussion of the strengths and weaknesses of social constructivism (e.g. Ruggie 1998; Wendt 1999; Risse 2000; Green 2002; Sending 2002) is not my purpose here, and I do not choose to follow this avenue of inquiry.

1 The power of globalization

1 This chapter was originally presented as a keynote address at the symposium 'Regional Policies in Europe – The Knowledge Age: Managing Global, Regional and Local Interdependencies', University of Graz, Austria, 21 September 2001. The discussion revisits and extends core arguments introduced in Mittelman (2000) and Mittelman and Norani (2001). Unless otherwise specified, all references herein to globalization or contemporary globalization shall mean the dominant neoliberal variant, to be delineated in this and ensuing chapters.
2 As is well known, the concept of power pervades the study of politics and the scholarly literature on it is vast (see, among other sources, Gaventa 1980; Wrong 1980; Lukes 1986; Dowding 1996; Hindess 1996).

2 Mapping globalization

1 Unbeknownst to me while writing this chapter, the journal *American Behavioral Scientist* 44, 10 (June 2001) devoted a special issue to this same theme, though quite differently from what is attempted here.

3 Globalization: an ascendant paradigm?

1 The literature (e.g. Appadurai 1996; Beck 2000; Giddens 2000) suggests a number of different ways to come to grips with what constitutes globalization.
2 This section builds on Mittelman (1997).
3 I have the strong impression, but cannot 'prove', that international studies scholars, with notable exceptions (e.g. Der Derian 1995; Peterson 1992; Sylvester 1994; Walker 1993), have been more insular in the face of incursions from postmodernism and poststructuralism than have those in the other social sciences.
4 Recognition of this pluralism may be found in both the name of the series in which this book appears and the title of the journal *Globalizations*. See http://www.tandf.co.uk/journals/titles/14747731.asp

5   In thinking about these issues, an impressive start is provided by Michael Burawoy
    (2000), Louise Amoore and Paul Langley (2001), and André Drainville (2003).

4 Critical globalization studies

1   I owe a debt of gratitude to William I. Robinson and Richard Appelbaum for inviting
    me to write this essay and present it at the conference 'Towards a Critical Globalization
    Studies: New Directions, Continuing Debates, and Neglected Topics', University of
    California, Santa Barbara, 1–4 May 2003.
2   There are infrastructures as well, such as the San Francisco-based International Forum
    on Globalization. In addition, since 2001, the World Social Forum (WSF), which has
    been meeting in Porto Alegre, Brazil, and then in Mumbai, India, thinks about ways to
    enact alternatives to neoliberal globalization.
3   'Can the subaltern speak?' is a theme elaborated by Gayatri Chakravorty Spivak (1990)
    and other postcolonial critics.
4   Compared to the Frankfurt School thinkers, who studied capitalism and mass society
    and sought critical distance in order to develop insight before translating theory into
    political interventions, the globalization critic is less apt to make the initial maneuver of
    political disengagement.
5   This emphasis is a corrective to an earlier generation of globalization studies, including
    my own work, which underemphasized the military factor as a motor of contemporary
    globalization.

5 Ideologies and the globalization agenda

1   I am grateful to Manfred B. Steger for inviting me to write this chapter, originally
    a paper presented at the conference on 'Ideological Dimensions of Globalization',
    Globalization Research Center, University of Hawai'i-Manoa, Honolulu, Hawai'i,
    9–12 December 2002.
2   Rewarded with recognition (e.g. on talk shows) and prizes for their contributions, many
    star policy intellectuals could be named, such as the Princeton economist Paul
    Krugman, a columnist who, without challenging the principles of neoliberalism,
    uncovers its baneful effects for the *New York Times*, an organ of power sometimes referred
    to as the fourth branch of the US government.
3   Right-wing populist and anarchist ideologies of globalization are probed in Mark
    Rupert (2000) and Steger (2002).
4   Stiglitz overextends himself in presenting a vast array of case studies. For him, like the
    World Bank and IMF, Uganda is a poster child. To be sure, the Yoweri Museveni
    government brought peace (except in the north) after years of dictatorships, helped
    spur economic growth, extended education without user fees, and improved health
    care, including a campaign to fight AIDS. Stiglitz waxes enthusiastic about these
    achievements without noting that while receiving substantial infusions of international
    funds, Museveni enforced his idea of a 'no party democracy', maintained a huge
    defense budget, and sent his military to loot the Democratic Republic of the Congo.
    Similarly, Stiglitz tells half the story when he claims that Malaysian Prime Minister
    Mahathir's capital controls were an effective response to the 1997–8 Asian economic
    crisis (which, as I have argued, was in fact a globalization crisis). Stiglitz is right as far as
    he goes, but either overlooks or does not know that investors and traders maneuvered
    around the controls and that others negotiated deals with the government. In any event,
    Mahathir, hardly a practitioner of good governance, lifted the controls after one year
    and sought to bolster Malaysia's rentier capitalism. The point here is that Stiglitz fails
    to get his stories right. (For an extended evaluation of Stiglitz's book, see my review in
    New Political Economy, 9, No. 1 (March): 129–33).

5   Similarly, Stiglitz (2002: 76, 242, 252) calls for 'a transformation of society', but the meaning is unspecified.

6 'Common-sense' representations of globalization protests

1   This chapter is a substantially modified version of a paper presented at the annual conference of the Political Economy of the World-System Section of the American Sociological Association, Georgetown University, Washington, DC, 25–6 April 2003. The term 'globalization' protests – not 'antiglobalization' protests or movement – is adopted here. The drawbacks to the term 'antiglobalization' are discussed in Chapters 1 and 4, and many protesters are in favor of some aspects of globalization (more information, new technology, productivity gains, etc.) but not others.

2   IndyMedia Centers provide an outlet for alternative media and independent writers. IndyMedia offer a database of globalization protests as seen by the participants (Kidd forthcoming).

3   In standard parlance, the terms North and South, or global North and global South, designate the divide between the developed and developing countries, although there are significant differences in levels of development within each of these categories. In fact, globalization, involves remaking the geoeconomic landscape, the changing contours showing substantial unevenness and irregularity (Dicken 2003: 509–12).

4   We are indebted to Priya Dixit for superb research assistance and Assen Assenov for help using SPSS. We also owe thanks to the students who administered the survey on 20 April 2002: Sean Andrews, David Bario, Rebecca Culbert, Enrique Gonzalez, Kelly McCarthy, David Murtha, Allison Halprin, Mvuselelo P. Ngcoya, Sarah Ploskon, Assel Rustemova, Meena Sharify-Funk, and Julianne Zuber.

5   All findings are drawn from the survey; however, in some instances tables are presented to clarify more intricate evidence.

6   These results closely parallel those of Vasi (n.d.: 17).

7   Lichbach (2002: 43), for example, reported that at most 3,000 out of 50,000 protestors came from beyond the US and Canada.

8   Not surprisingly, these data almost reverse those generated by Rosenau and his colleagues in their survey of the elites depicted as 'cutting-edge globalizers' (Rosenau *et al.* forthcoming).

9   To gauge their degree of participation, interviewees were assigned a numerical value based on the nature of their organizational involvement: officeholder (3), active member (2), inactive member (1), and non-member (0). Inasmuch as many interviewees are involved in more than one organization, the values were added across the nine types of organizations surveyed to construct an overall index of their organizational activism. These included antinuclear, civil rights, environmental, gay and lesbian rights, global justice, labor, peace, and women's rights.

10   Interviewees were given a numerical value for their degree of participation in global justice protests: organizer (4), protester (3), petitioner (2), follower of the events in the news (1), and nonparticipant (0). Insofar as many interviewees are involved in more than one protest, these values were added across seven major protests in the US and abroad to establish an overall index of their organizational activism. The protests include Seattle, Stockholm, Washington (April 2000 and September 2001), Quebec City, and Genoa.

11   Even this correspondence may be a function of the intersection of Northern media and Northern protests, and may not capture the composition of protests in the global South,

which might draw on different class, race, and gender constituencies. Without comparative research, we cannot ascertain whether these results reflect the Northern face of a more diverse global movement.

7   Bringing in micro-encounters

1   A preliminary draft of this chapter was presented at the conference on 'Globalisation, Cultures and Inequalities – in Honour of the Work of the Late Professor Ishak Shari', National University of Malaysia, Bangi, Malaysia, 19–21 August 2002.
2   For research assistance on Foucault's concept of resistance, I owe an enormous debt of gratitude to Peter Howard (Research note 10 October 2000).
3   Elsewhere (2000: 166–75 with Christine B. N. Chin, 182–5, 200–1), I have assessed various approaches to resistance, including Polanyi's, Gramsci's, Scott's. So as not to repeat myself, suffice it to say that the other perspectives deepen understanding of resistance and offer powerful tools for analysis, but differ in important respects from what is undertaken here.
4   The topics selected by the other students were 'Emerging Spaces of Resistance: The Situation of Immigrants in Japan', 'Voting Rights of Foreign Residents in Japan', and 'WTO and [the] Timber Industry.' To stretch my point, it could be argued that the projects on immigration and on decisions concerning who is a legal member or not of the body politic are also about the regulation of the body. Although the media and conventional social science cover these same topics, it is noteworthy that at least half of the student teams chose themes in line with Foucault's analysis. The students could have possibly arrived at the same point through another route, but the *concentration* on themes resonant with a Foucaultian interpretation is striking.
5   When Bové and other farmers smashed a McDonald's restaurant, they were protesting the US government's decision to impose sanctions on imported French delicacies such as foie gras and Roquefort cheese, a local product on farms in Millau. The application of sanctions followed the refusal by France and other European countries to permit the import of American beef treated with growth hormones. At his trial, Bové explained:

> When was there a public debate on genetically modified organisms? When were farmers and consumers asked about this? Never. The decisions were taken at the level of the World Trade Organization (WTO), and state machinery complies with the law of market forces . . .
>
> (Bové 2000)

He added:

> [T]he greatest concerns surrounding genetically modified maize are equally important for human health as for nature. Novartis' Bt maize is associated with multiple long-term risks because of the presence of the three introduced genes. Even the director of Novartis recognizes that a 'zero-risk' simply doesn't exist. Is this an admission of powerlessness . . ?
>
> (Bové 2000)

6   Scholars, research scientists, journalists, and activists have compiled a piecemeal literature on these themes. It includes the vast and multifaceted writings on the many issues about globalization raised by the feminist movement in Japan (e.g. 'The Women's Movement Then and Now' 1995; Buckley 1997; Matsui 1999). There are also detailed analyses of resistance to genetically modified food (Yasuda 2000; and at the Consumers Union of Japan Web site http://jca.apc.org/nishoren) as well as against the free trade guidelines of the WTO and the liberalization of imported foods (Oono1999; Mizuhara1999). On the rice issue, there is Ohnuki-Tierney (1993), and for other

facets of globalization in Japan, most notably Eades, Gill, and Befu (2000) and Clammer (2001).

7 For information on this campaign on crimes against women, see http://www1.jca.apc.org/vaww-net-japan/english

8 Alterglobalization

1 The beginning of this chapter incorporates some passages from and develops my previous formulations on alternative globalization (Mittelman 1999, 2000, 2003).

References

Abdul Rahman Embong. (2002) *State-Led Modernization and the New Middle Class in Malaysia*, New York: Palgrave Macmillan.

Ake, Claude. (1996) *Democracy and Development in Africa*, Washington, DC: Brookings Institution.

Alker, Hayward R. Jr. (1996) *Rediscoveries and Reformulations: Humanistic Methods for International Studies*, Cambridge, UK: Cambridge University Press.

Amoore, Louise. (ed.) (forthcoming) *The Global Resistance Reader*, London: Routledge.

Amoore, Louise and Langley, Paul. (2001) 'Experiencing Globalization: Active Teaching and Learning in International Political Economy', *International Studies Perspectives*, 2, No. 1 (February): 15–32.

Appadurai, Arjun. (1996) *Modernity at Large: Cultural Dimensions of Globalization*, Minneapolis: University of Minnesota Press.

Arai, Sanri, Inoue, Yoshinobu, Otsuki, Makikio, Takayangi, Mari and Yamagishi, Naoyuki. (2000) 'The Resistance to Genetically Modified Foods in Japan: A Case Study of the Resistance to Globalization', Unpublished.

Aristotle. (1962) *The Politics of Aristotle*, trans. and ed. Ernest Barker, New York: Oxford University Press.

Arrighi, Giovanni and Silver, Beverly J. (1999) *Chaos and Governance in the Modern World System*, Minneapolis: University of Minnesota Press.

A. T. Kearney, Inc. (2003) 'Measuring Globalization: Who's Up, Who's Down?', *Foreign Policy*, 134 (January–February): 60–72.

Ayres, Jeffrey and Tarrow, Sidney. (2002) 'The Shifting Grounds for Transnational Civic Activity', Social Science Research Council. Online. Available: <http://www.ssrc.org/sept11/essays/ayres.htm> (accessed 15 December 2003).

Baker, Andrew. (2000) 'Globalization and the British "Residual State"', in Richard Stubbs and Geoffrey R.D. Underhill (eds) *Political Economy and the Changing Global Order*, second edn, Don Mills, Ontario: Oxford University Press, 362–72.

Ball, Terence. (1976) 'From Paradigms to Research Programs: Toward a Post-Kuhnian Political Science', *American Journal of Political Science*, 20, No.1 (February): 151–77.

Barlow, Maude and Clarke, Tony. (2001) *Global Showdown: How the New Activists Are Fighting Global Corporate Rule*, Toronto: Stoddart.

Barnes, Barry. (1982) *T. S. Kuhn and Social Science*, New York: Columbia University Press.

Beck, Ulrich. (2000) *What Is Globalization?* trans. Patrick Camiller, Cambridge, UK: Polity Press.

Bello, Walden. (2002) *Deglobalization: Ideas for a New World Economy*, London: Zed Books.

Benería, Lourdes. (2003) *Gender, Development, and Globalization: Economics as if All People Mattered*, New York: Routledge.

Bhagwati, Jagdish. (2002) 'Coping with Antiglobalization: A Trilogy of Discontents', *Foreign Affairs*, 81, No. 1 (January–February): 2–7.

Bond, Patrick. (1995) 'Under the Microscope: The ANC in Power', *Southern Africa Report* (Toronto), 10, No. 3: 3–7.

Bové, José. (2000) 'José Bové's Statement to Court. Southeast Michigan Coalition on Occupational Safety and Health', Online. Available: <www.semcosh.org/Jose%20Bove. htm> (accessed 27 January 2004).

Bové, José and Dufour, François. (2000) *Le monde n'est pas une marchandise: Des paysans contre la malbouffe* [The World Is Not for Sale: Farmers against Junk Food], Paris: Éditions La Découverte.

Braudel, Fernand. (1980) 'History and the Social Sciences: The *Longue Durée*', in *On History*, trans. Sarah Matthews, Chicago: University of Chicago Press, 25–54.

——(1980) *On History*, trans. Sarah Matthews, Chicago: University of Chicago Press.

——(1990) *Afterthoughts on Material Civilization and Capitalism*, trans. Patricia Ranum, Baltimore: Johns Hopkins University Press.

——(1994) *A History of Civilizations*, trans. Richard Mayne, New York: Penguin.

Broad, Robin. (ed.) (2002) *Global Backlash: Citizen Initiatives for a Just World Economy*, Lanham, MD: Rowman and Littlefield.

Brzezinski, Zbigniew. (1997) *The Grand Chessboard: American Primacy and Its Geostrategic Imperatives*, New York: Basic Books.

Buckley, Sandra. (1997) *Broken Silence: Voices of Japanese Feminism*, Berkeley: University of California Press.

Burawoy, Michael. (2000) *Global Ethnography: Forces, Connections, and Imaginations in a Postmodern World*, Berkeley: University of California Press.

Carr, Edward H. (1964) *The Twenty Years' Crisis, 1919–1939*, New York: Harper and Row.

Castells, Manuel. (1996) *The Rise of the Network Society*, Oxford: Blackwell.

Caton, Steven C. (1999) *Lawrence of Arabia: A Film's Anthropology*, Berkeley: University of California Press.

Cerny, Philip G. (1996) 'Globalization and Other Stories: The Search for a New Paradigm for International Relations', *International Journal*, 51 (Autumn): 617–37.

Cheru, Fantu. (2002) *African Renaissance: Roadmaps to the Challenge of Globalization*, London: Zed Books.

Clammer, John. (2001) *Japan and Its Others*, Melbourne: Trans Pacific Press.

Clark, Ian. (1999) G*lobalization and International Relations Theory*, Oxford: Oxford University Press.

Consumers Union of Japan. Online. Available: <http://jca.apc.org/nishoren> (accessed 14 December 2003).

Cosslett, Tess, Easton, Alison and Summerfield, Penny. (eds) (1996) *Women, Power, and Resistance: An Introduction to Women's Studies*, Philadelphia: Open University Press.

Council for the Development of Economic and Social Research in Africa. (1998) 'Social Sciences and Globalisation in Africa', *CODESRIA Bulletin*, 2 (December): 3–6.

——(2002) '10th General Assembly: Africa in the New Millennium', Special Issue, *CODESRIA Bulletin*, 3 and 4.

Cox, Michael. (ed.) (2000) *E. H. Carr: A Critical Appraisal*, London and New York: Palgrave.

Cox, Robert W. (1979) 'Ideologies and the New International Economic Order: Reflections on Some Recent Literature', *International Organization*, 33, No. 2 (Spring): 257–302.

——(1986) 'Social Forces, States, and World Orders: Beyond International Relations Theory', in Robert Keohane (ed.) *Neorealism and Its Critics*, New York: Columbia University Press, 204–54.

——(1987) *Production, Power and World Order: Social Forces in the Making of History*, New York: Columbia University Press.

——(1996) 'A Perspective on Globalization', in James H. Mittelman (ed.) *Globalization: Critical Reflections*, Boulder, CO: Lynne Rienner, 21–30.

——with Michael G. Schechter. (2002) *The Political Economy of a Plural World: Critical Reflections on Power, Morals and Civilization*, London: Routledge.

'Cultural Loss Seen as Languages Fade' (1999) *New York Times*, 16 May.

Danaher, Kevin. (ed.) (2001) *Democratizing the Global Economy: The Battle against the World Bank and the International Monetary Fund*, Monroe, ME: Common Courage Press.

Der Derian, James. (ed.) (1995) *International Theory: Critical Investigations*, New York: New York University Press.

Dicken, Peter. (2003) *Global Shift: Reshaping the Global Economic Map in the 21st Century*, fourth edn, New York: Guilford.

Dowding, Keith. (1996) *Power*, Minneapolis: University of Minnesota Press.

Drainville, André C. (2003) 'Critical Pedagogy for the Current Moment: Learning from the Avant-Garde to Teach Globalization from Experiences', *International Studies Perspectives*, 4, No. 3 (August): 231–49.

Dreyfus, Hubert L. and Rabinow, Paul. (1982) *Michel Foucault: Beyond Structuralism and Hermeneutics*, Chicago: University of Chicago Press.

Eades, Jeremy Seymour, Gill, Tom and Befu, Harumi. (eds) (2000) *Globalization and Social Change in Contemporary Japan*, Melbourne: Trans Pacific Press.

Falk, Richard. (1999) *Predatory Globalization: A Critique*, Cambridge, UK: Polity Press.

——(2003) 'Globalization-from-Below: An Innovative Politics of Difference', in Richard Sandbrook (ed.) *Civilizing Globalization: A Survival Guide*, Albany: State University of New York Press, 189–205.

Ferguson, Yale H. and Rosenau, James N. (2003) 'Superpowerdom before and after September 11, 2001: A Postinternational Perspective', paper presented at the Annual Meeting of the International Studies Association, Portland, OR, February.

Ferrer, Aldo. (1997) *Hechos y Ficciones de la Globalización* [Facts and Fictions of Globalization], Buenos Aires: Fondo de Cultura Economica [Collection of Economic Writings].

Fisher, Sue and Davis, Kathy. (eds) (1993) *Negotiating at the Margins: The Gendered Discourses of Power and Resistance*, New Brunswick: Rutgers University Press.

Foucault, Michel. (1977) *Discipline and Punish: The Birth of the Prison*, trans. A. Sheridan, New York: Pantheon Books.

——(1980) *Power/Knowledge: Selected Interviews and Other Writings, 1972–1977*, trans. and ed. C. Gordon *et al.*, New York: Pantheon Books.

——(1982) 'The Subject and Power', Afterword in Hubert L. Dreyfus and Paul Rabinow (eds) *Michel Foucault: Beyond Structuralism and Hermeneutics*, Chicago: University of Chicago Press, 208–26.

——(1990) *The History of Sexuality. Volume I: An Introduction*, trans. R. Hurley, New York: Random House.

Friedman, Jonathan. (1994) *Cultural Identity and Global Process*, Thousand Oaks, CA: Sage.

Friedman, Thomas L. (1999) *The Lexus and the Olive Tree: Understanding Globalization*, New York: Farrar, Straus & Giroux.

Gaventa, John. (1980) *Power and Powerlessness: Quiescence and Rebellion in an Appalachian Valley*, Urbana: University of Illinois Press.

Geuss, Raymond. (1981) *The Idea of a Critical Theory: Habermas and the Frankfurt School*, Cambridge, UK: Cambridge University Press.

Giddens, Anthony. (1990) *The Consequences of Modernity*, Cambridge, UK: Polity Press.

——(2000) *Runaway World: How Globalization Is Reshaping Our Lives*, New York: Routledge.

Gill, Stephen and Mittelman, James H. (eds) (1997) *Innovation and Transformation in International Studies*, Cambridge, UK: Cambridge University Press.

Gills, Barry K. (ed.) (2000) *Globalization and the Politics of Resistance*, London: Macmillan and New York: St. Martin's.

Gilpin, Robert. (2000) T*he Challenge of Global Capitalism: The World Economy in the 21st Century*, Princeton: Princeton University Press.

Glick Schiller, Nina. (1999) 'Citizens in Transnational Nation-States: The Asian Experience', in Kris Olds *et al.* (eds) *Globalization and the Asia Pacific: Contested Territories*, London: Routledge, 202–18.

Gómez, J. M. (2000) *Política e democracia em tempos de globalização* [Politics and Democracy in the Era of Globalization], Petrópolis, RJ, Brazil: Editora Vozes.

Gordon, David. (1988) 'The Global Economy: New Edifice or Crumbling Foundations?' *New Left Review*, 168 (March/April): 24–64.

Gramsci, Antonio. (1971) *Selections from the Prison Notebooks*, trans. and ed. Quintin Hoare and Geoffrey Nowell Smith, London: Lawrence and Wishart.

——(2000) *The Gramsci Reader: Selected Writings 1916–1935*, ed. David Forgacs, New York: New York University Press.

Gray, John. (1998) *False Dawn: The Delusions of Global Capitalism*, London: Granta Books.

——(2001) 'The Era of Globalisation Is Over', *New Statesman*, 24 September: 25–7.

Green, Daniel M. (ed.) (2002) *Constructivism and Comparative Politics*, Armonk, NY: M.E. Sharpe.

Guillén, Mauro F. (2001) 'Is Globalization Civilizing, Destructive or Feeble? A Critique of Five Key Debates in the Social-Science Literature', *Annual Review of Sociology*, 27: 235–60.

Harding, Sandra. (1991) *Whose Science? Whose Knowledge? Thinking from Women's Lives*, Ithaca, NY: Cornell University Press.

Hardt, Michael and Negri, Antonio. (2000) *Empire*, Cambridge, MA: Harvard University Press.

Harvey, David. (1990) *The Condition of Postmodernity*, Oxford: Basil Blackwell.

——(1999) *Limits to Capital*, London: Verso.

Hekman, Susan. (1997) 'Truth and Method: Feminist Standpoint Theory Revisited', *Journal of Women in Culture and Society*, 22, No. 2 (Winter): 341–65.

Held, David. (1995) *Democracy and the Global Order: From the Modern State to Cosmopolitan Governance*, Stanford, CA: Stanford University Press.

Held, David and McGrew, Anthony. (2002) *Globalization/Anti-Globalization*, Cambridge, UK: Polity Press.

Held, David and McGrew, Anthony. (eds) (2003) *Global Transformations Reader*, second edn, Malden, MA: Polity Press.

Held, David *et al.* (1999) *Global Transformations: Politics, Economics and Culture*, Cambridge, UK: Polity Press.

Hettne, Björn. (2002a) 'Discourses on Utopianism: Polanyi and the Search for World Order', Unpublished.

——(2002b) 'Globalisation, Regionalisation and Security: The Asian Experience', *European Journal of Development Research*, 14, No. 1 (June): 28–46.

Hettne, Björn and Odén, Bertil. (eds) (2002) *Global Governance in the 21st Century: Alternative Perspectives on World Order*, Stockholm: Almqvist & Wiksell International.

Hindess, Barry. (1996) *Discourses of Power: From Hobbes to Foucault*, Oxford: Blackwell.

Hirst, Paul and Thompson, Grahame. (1999) *Globalization in Question: The International Economy and the Possibilities of Governance*, second edn, Cambridge, UK: Polity Press.

Hotta, Masahiko. (2000) President, Alter Trade, Inc. Interview by James H. Mittelman, Tokyo, 5 December 2000.

——(forthcoming) 'Bananas: The Negros Alternative', in Robin Murray and Pauline Tiffen (eds) *Understanding and Expanding Fair Trade*, Vol. 2, London: TWIN.

Howard, Peter. (2000) 'Research note', 10 October, unpublished.

Ikeda, Hiroaki, Rello, Reis Lopez and Lundh, Janne-Magnus. (2000) 'Globalization's Effects on Japanese Women and Their Reactions', Unpublished.

Imam, R.H. (2001) 'Research note', Unpublished.

Imig, Doug and Tarrow, Sidney. (2001) *Contentious Europeans: Protest and Politics in an Emerging Polity*, Lanham, MD: Rowman and Littlefield.

Inoue, Reiko. (2000) Member and former President, Pacific Asia Resource Center. Correspondence with James H. Mittelman, 16 December.

Jessop, Bob. (1997) Comments at the Workshop on The Logic(s) of Globalisation, National University of Singapore, Singapore, 3–5 December.

——(1999) 'Reflections on Globalisation and Its (Il)logics(s)', in Kris Olds *et al.* (eds) *Globalisation and the Asia-Pacific: Contested Territories*, London and New York: Routledge, 19–38.

Kaldor, Mary. (1999) *New and Old Wars: Organized Violence in a Global Era*, Stanford, CA: Stanford University Press.

Kaneko, Masaru. (1999) *Han Gurouburizumu: Shijou Kaiku no Senryakuteki Shikou* [Anti-globalism: Strategic Thinking on Market Reforms], Tokyo: Iwanami Shoten.

Keck, Margaret E. and Sikkink, Kathryn. (1998) *Activists beyond Borders: Advocacy Networks in International Politics*, Ithaca, NY: Cornell University Press.

Keohane, Robert O. (1984) *After Hegemony: Cooperation and Discord in the World Political Economy*, Princeton: Princeton University Press.

Keohane, Robert O. and Nye, Joseph S. Jr. (1977) *Power and Interdependence: World Politics in Transition*, Boston and Toronto: Little, Brown.

——(1998) 'Power and Interdependence in the Information Age', New York: Council on Foreign Relations.

——(2000) 'Globalization: What's New? What's Not? (And So What?)', *Foreign Policy*, 118 (Spring): 104–20.

Khor, Martin. (2001) *Rethinking Globalization: Critical Policy Issues and Policy Choices*, New York: Palgrave, St. Martin's Press.

Kidd, Dorothy. (forthcoming) 'Indymedia.org and the Global Social Justice Movement', in Andy Opel and Donnalyn Pompper (eds) *Representing Resistance: Media, Civil Disobedience & the Global Justice Movement*, Westport, CT: Greenwood.

Klein, Naomi. (1999) *No Logo*, New York: Picador.

——(2002) *Fences and Windows: Dispatches from the Front Lines of the Globalization Debate*, New York: Picador.

Knox, Paul and Agnew, John. (1998) *The Geography of the World Economy*, third edn, London: Edward Arnold.

Kontani, Ayako, Kawada, Takahiro and Uemura, Tomohiro. (2000) 'WTO and Farming Product (Rice)', Unpublished.

Kuhn, Thomas S. (1970) *The Structure of Scientific Revolutions*, second edn, Chicago: University of Chicago Press.

——(1977a) *The Essential Tension: Selected Studies in Scientific Tradition and Change*, Chicago: University of Chicago Press.

——(1977b) 'Second Thoughts on Paradigms', in Frederick Suppe (ed.) *The Structure of Scientific Theories*, second edn, Urbana: University of Illinois Press, 459–82.

Lakatos, Imre. (1970) 'Falsification and the Methodology of Scientific Research Programmes', in Imre Lakatos and Alan Musgrave (eds) *Criticism and the Growth of Knowledge*, Cambridge, UK: Cambridge University Press, 91–196.

Lapid, Yosef. (1989) 'The Third Debate: On the Prospects of International Theory in a Post-positivist Era', *International Studies Quarterly*, 33, No. 3 (September): 235–54.

Laslett, Barbara, Brenner, Johanna and Arat, Yesim (eds) (1995) *Rethinking the Political: Gender, Resistance, and the State*, Chicago: University of Chicago Press.

Leite, Paulo Moreira. (1996) 'Males Globalizados', trans. Lillian Duarte. *Veja*, 29, No. 9 (28 February): 24–5.

Lemert, Charles. (1993) 'Social Theory: Its Uses and Pleasures', in Charles Lemert (ed.) *Social Theory: The Multicultural and Classical Readings*, Boulder, CO: Westview, 1–24.

Lichbach, Mark Irving. (2002) 'Global Order and Local Resistance: Structure, Culture, and Rationality in the Battle of Seattle', Unpublished.

Lukes, Steven. (ed.) (1986) *Power*, New York: New York University Press.

McAdam, Doug, Tarrow, Sidney and Tilly, Charles. (2001) *Dynamics of Contention*, Cambridge, UK: Cambridge University Press.

McMichael, Philip. (2004) *Development and Social Change: A Global Perspective*, third edn, Thousand Oaks, CA: Pine Forge Press.

Machiavelli, Niccolò. (1985) *The Prince*, trans. H .C. Mansfield, Chicago: University of Chicago Press.

'Mapping Globalization', (2001) Special Issue, *American Behavioral Scientist*, 44, No. 10 (June).

Matsui, Yayori. (1999) *Women in the New Asia: From Pain to Power*, trans. N. Toyokawa, London: Zed Books.

Melucci, Alberto. (1985) 'The Symbolic Challenge of Contemporary Movements', *Social Research*, 52, No. 4: 789–914.

——(1996) *Challenging Codes: Collective Action in the Information Age*, New York: Cambridge University Press.

Micklethwait, John and Wooldridge, Adrian. (2000) *A Future Perfect: The Challenge and Hidden Promise of Globalization*, New York: Crown Business.

Milanovic, Branko. (2002) 'True World Income Distribution, 1988 and 1993: First Calculation Based on Household Surveys Alone', *Economic Journal*, 112, No. 476: 51–92.

Mittelman, James H. (1997) 'Rethinking Innovation in International Studies: Global Transformation at the Turn of the Millennium', in Stephen Gill and James H. Mittelman (eds) *Innovation and Transformation in International Studies*, Cambridge, UK: Cambridge University Press, 248–63.

——(1999) *The Future of Globalization*, Bangi, Malaysia: Penerbit Universiti Kebangsaan Malaysia [National University of Malaysia Press].

——(2000) *The Globalization Syndrome: Transformation and Resistance*, Princeton: Princeton University Press.

——(2003) 'Alternative Globalization', in Richard Sandbrook (ed.) *Civilizing Globalization*, Albany: State University of New York Press, 237–51.

Mittelman, James H. and Norani Othman. (eds) (2001) *Capturing Globalization*, London and New York: Routledge.

Mizuhara, Hiroko. (1999) 'Liberalization of Imported Foods', *AMPO: Japan–Asia Quarterly Review*, 28, No. 4: 31–3.

Muto, Ichiyo. (2000) Member, People's Plan Study Group. Interview by James H. Mittelman. Tokyo, 7 December 2000.

Nakatani, Yoshikazu. (n.d.) 'Global Democracy: A Japanese Perspective', unpublished.

Nederveen Pieterse, Jan. (2004) *Globalization and Culture: Global Mélange*, Lanham, MD: Rowman and Littlefield.

Norani Othman and Mandal, Sumit Kumar. (eds) (2000) *Malaysia Menangani Globalisasi: Peserata atau Mangasi?* [Malaysia Responding to Globalization: Participants or Victims?], Bangi, Malaysia: Penerbit Universiti Kebangsaan Malaysia [National University of Malaysia Press].

O'Brien, Robert *et al.* (2000) *Contesting Global Governance: Multilateral Economic Institutions and Global Social Movements*, Cambridge, UK: Cambridge University Press.

Ohmae, Kenichi. (1999) *The Borderless World: Power and Strategy in an Interlinked Economy*, New York: Harper Business.

Ohnuki-Tierney, Emiko. (1993) *Rice as Self: Japanese Identities through Time*, Princeton: Princeton University Press.

Olds, Kris. (2001) *Globalization and Urban Change: Capital, Culture, and Pacific Rim Mega-Projects*, Oxford and New York: Oxford University Press.

Olds, Kris *et al.* (eds) (1999) *Globalisation and the Asia-Pacific: Contested Territories*, London: Routledge.

Oono, Kazuoki. (1999) 'Agricultural Deregulation at Its Final Stage', *AMPO: Japan–Asia Quarterly Review*, 28, No. 4: 28–30.

Overbeek, Henk. (2001) 'Transnational Historical Materialism: Theories of Transnational Class Formation and World Order', in Ronen Palan (ed.) *The New Global Political Economy: Theorizing and Approaches*, London: Routledge, 168–84.

Panitch, Leo. (1996) 'Rethinking the Role of the State', in James H. Mittelman (ed.) *Globalization: Critical Reflections*, Boulder, CO: Lynne Rienner, 83–113.

Patomäki, Heikki. (2003) 'Problems of Democratizing Global Governance: Time, Space and the Emancipatory Process', *European Journal of International Relations*, 9, No. 3: 347–76.

Patomäki, Heikki and Teivainen, Teivo. (2002) *Global Democracy Initiatives: The Art of the Possible*, Helsinki: Network Institute for Global Democratization Working Paper 2.

Paulson, Henry. (2001) 'The Gospel of Globalisation', *Financial Times*, 13 November, p. 25.

Peck, Jamie and Yeung, Henry Wai-chung. (2003) *Remaking the Global Economy: Economic-Geographical Perspectives*, London: Sage.

People's Plan for The Twenty-First Century. (2000) Online. Available: <http://www.hr-alliance.org/pp21/channel2.html> 28 October. (Inactive)

Peterson, V. Spike. (ed.) (1992) *Gendered States: Feminist (Re)Visions of International Relations*, Boulder, CO: Lynne Rienner.

Peterson, V. Spike. (2003) *A Critical Rewriting of Global Political Economy: Integrating Reproductive, Productive, and Virtual Economies*, London: Routledge.

Pfaff, William. (2000) 'Globalization Is Discredited', *Japan Times*, 29 February.

Pickett, Brent L. (1996) 'Foucault and the Politics of Resistance', *Polity*, 28, No 4: 445–66.

Pile, Steve and Keith, Michael (eds) (1997) *Geographies of Resistance*, London and New York: Routledge.

Podestà, Bruno *et al.* (eds) (2000) *Ciudadanía y mundialización regional: La sociedad civil ante la integración regional* [Urbanism and Regional Globalization: Civil Society before Regional Integration], Madrid: CIDEAL.

Polanyi, Karl. (1957) *The Great Transformation: The Political and Economic Origins of Our Time*, Boston: Beacon Press.

Puchala, Donald J. (2000) 'Marking a Weberian Moment: Our Discipline Looks Ahead', *International Studies Perspectives*, 1, No. 2 (August): 133–44.

——(2001) Personal correspondence with James H. Mittelman, 30 January.

Rawls, John. (1993) *Political Liberalism*, New York: Columbia University Press.

Risse, Thomas. (2000) 'Let's Argue: Communicative Action in World Politics', *International Organization*, 54, No. 1 (Winter): 1–39.

Ritzer, George. (2000) *The McDonaldization of Society*, Thousand Oaks, CA: Pine Forge Press.

Robertson, Roland. (1992) *Globalization: Social Theory and Global Culture*, Newbury Park, CA: Sage.

Robertson, Roland and White, Kathleen. (eds) (2003) *Globalization: Critical Concepts in Sociology*, London: Routledge.

Robinson, William I. (2001) 'Social Theory and Globalization: The Rise of a Transnational State', *Theory and Society*, 30, No. 2 (April): 157–200.

Rodrik, Dani. (1997) *Has Globalization Gone Too Far?* Washington, DC: Institute for International Economics.

Rosenau, James N. (1997) *Along the Domestic–Foreign Frontier: Exploring Governance in a Turbulent World*, Cambridge, UK: Cambridge University Press.

Rosenau, James N. *et al.* (forthcoming) 'On the Cutting Edge of Globalization', unpublished.

Rosow, Stephen J. (1999) 'Globalization/Democratic Theory: The Politics of Representation of Post-Cold War Political Space', paper presented at the annual meeting of the International Studies Association, Washington, DC, February.

Ross, Stephanie. (2003) 'Is This What Democracy Looks Like? The Politics of the Anti-Globalization Movement in North America', in Leo Panitch and Colin Leys (eds) *Socialist Register*, London: Merlin Press, 281–304.

Routledge, Paul. (2000) 'Our Resistance Will Be as Transnational as Capital: Convergence Space and Strategy in Globalising Resistance', *Geojournal*, 52, No. 1: 25–53.

Ruggie, John G. (1993) 'Territoriality and Beyond: Problematizing Modernity in International Relations', *International Organization*, 47, No. 1 (Winter): 139–74.

——(1998) *Constructing the World Polity: Essays on International Institutionalization*, London: Routledge.

Rupert, Mark. (2000) *Ideologies of Globalization: Contending Visions of a New World Order*, London: Routledge.

Sabihah Osman. (2001) 'Globalization and Democratization: The Response of the Indigenous Peoples of Sarawak', in James H. Mittelman and Norani Othman (eds) *Capturing Globalization*, London and New York: Routledge, 77–91.

Said, Edward W. (1979) *Orientalism*, New York: Vintage.

Sakamoto, Yoshikazu. (2001) Professor emeritus, University of Tokyo. Correspondence with James H. Mittelman, 5 January.

——(ed.) (1994) *Global Transformation: Challenges to the State System*, Tokyo: United Nations University Press.

Sandbrook, Richard. (ed.) (2003) *Civilizing Globalization: A Survival Guide*, Albany, NY: State University of New York Press.

Sassen, Saskia. (1996) *Losing Control? Sovereignty in an Age of Globalization*, New York: Columbia University Press.

——(1998) *Globalization and Its Discontents: Essays on the New Mobility of People and Money*, New York: The New Press.

——(2001) *The Global City: New York, London, Tokyo*, second edn, Princeton: Princeton University Press.

Scholte, Jan Aart. (1999) 'Globalisation: Prospects for a Paradigm Shift', in Martin Shaw (ed.) *Politics and Globalisation: Knowledge, Ethics and Agency*, London and New York: Routledge, 9–22.

——(2000) *Globalization: A Critical Introduction*, New York: St. Martin's Press.

Scott, James C. (1990) *Domination and the Arts of Resistance: Hidden Transcripts*, New Haven, CT: Yale University Press.

Sending, Ole Jacob. (2002) 'Constitution, Choice and Change: Problems with the 'Logic of Appropriateness' and Its Use in Constructionist Theory', *European Journal of International Relations*, 8, No. 4 (December): 443–71.

Seoane, José and Taddei, Emilio. (eds) (2001) *Resistencias mundiales (De Seattle a Porto Alegre)* [Global Resistance (From Seattle to Porto Alegre)], Buenos Aires: Consejo Latinamericano de Ciencias Sociales.

Sharp, Joanne P. *et al.* (eds) (2000) *Entanglements of Power: Geographies of Domination/Resistance*, London and New York: Routledge.

Shaw, Martin. (1994) *Global Society and International Relations: Sociological Concepts and Political Perspectives*, Cambridge, UK: Polity Press.

——(ed.) (1999) *Politics and Globalisation: Knowledge, Ethics and Agency*, London: Routledge.

Shotter, John. (1993) *Cultural Politics of Everyday Life: Social Constructionism, Rhetoric and Knowing of the Third Kind*, Toronto: University of Toronto Press.

Sinclair, Timothy J. (1994a) 'Between State and Market: Hegemony and Institutions of Collective Action under Conditions of International Capital Mobility', *Policy Sciences*, 27, No. 4: 447–66.

Sinclair, Timothy. (1994b) 'Passing Judgment: Credit Rating Processes as Regulatory Mechanisms of Governance in the Emerging World Order', *Review of International Political Economy*, 1, No. 1 (Spring): 133–59.

Sklair, Leslie. (1996) 'Who Are the Globalisers? A Study of Key Globalisers in Australia', *Journal of Australian Political Economy*, 38 (December): 1–30.

——2002. *Globalization: Capitalism and Its Alternatives*, third edn, Oxford: Oxford University Press.

Smith, Jackie. (2002) 'Globalizing Resistance: The Battle of Seattle and the Future of Social Movements', in Jackie Smith and Hank Johnston (eds) *Globalization and Resistance: Transnational Dimensions of Social Movements*, Lanham, MD: Rowman and Littlefield, 207–27.

Smith, Jackie, Chatfield, Charles and Pagnucco, Ron. (1997) *Transnational Social Movements and Global Politics: Solidarity beyond the State*, Syracuse, NY: Syracuse University Press.

Smith, Jackie and Johnston, Hank. (eds) (2002) *Globalization and Resistance: Transnational Dimensions of Social Movements*, Lanham, MD: Rowman and Littlefield.

Sorkin, Michael. (ed.) (1992) *Variations on a Theme Park: The New American City and the End of Public Space*, New York: Hill and Wang.

Soros, George. (2002) *George Soros on Globalization*, New York: Public Affairs.

Spivak, Gayatri Chakravorty. (1990) *The Post-Colonial Critic: Interviews, Strategies, Dialogues*, ed. Sarah Harasym, London: Routledge.

Starr, Amory. (2000) *Naming the Enemy: Anti-Corporate Movements Confront Globalization*, London: Zed Books.

——(2003) 'Is the North American Anti-Globalization Movement Racist? Critical Reflections', in Leo Panitch and Colin Leys (eds) *Socialist Register*, London: Merlin Press, 265–80.

Steger, Manfred B. (2002) *Globalism: The New Market Ideology*, Lanham, MD: Rowman and Littlefield.

—— (2003a) *Globalization: A Very Short Introduction*, New York: Oxford University Press.

—— (ed.) (2003b) *Rethinking Globalism*, Lanham, MD: Rowman and Littlefield.

Stern, Nicholas. (2000) *A Strategy for Development*, Washington, DC: World Bank.

Stiglitz, Joseph E. (2002) *Globalization and Its Discontents*, New York: W.W. Norton.

Strange, Susan. (1996) *The Retreat of the State: The Diffusion of Power in the World*, New York: Cambridge University Press

—— (1998) *Mad Money: When Markets Outgrow Governments*, Ann Arbor: University of Michigan Press.

Sylvester, Christine. (1994) *Feminist Theory and International Relations Theory in a Postmodern Era*, Cambridge, UK: Cambridge University Press.

Tabb, William K. (2001) *The Amoral Elephant: Globalization and the Struggle for Social Justice in the Twenty-First Century*, New York: Monthly Review Press.

Tarrow, Sidney. (2002) 'From Lumping to Splitting: Specifying Globalization and Resistance', in Jackie Smith and Hank Johnston (eds) *Globalization and Resistance: Transnational Dimensions of Social Movements*, Lanham, MD: Rowman and Littlefield, 229–49.

Taylor, Peter J. (1993) *Political Geography: World-Economy, Nation-State, and Locality*, New York: Wiley.

Taylor, Peter J., Johnston, Ronald J. and Watts, Michael. (1995) *Geographies of Global Change: Remapping the World in the Late Twentieth Century*, Oxford, UK: Blackwell.

Teeple, Gary. (1995) *Globalization and the Decline of Social Reform*, Atlantic Highlands, NJ: Humanities Press International.

Thrift, Nigel. (1996) *Spatial Formations*, London: Sage.

Tickner, J. Ann. (2001) *Gendering World Politics: Issues and Approaches in the Post-Cold War Era*, New York: Columbia University Press.

Tomlinson, John. (1999) *Globalization and Culture*, Chicago: University of Chicago Press.

Truehart, Charles. (1997) 'French Hold Proudly Fast to Benevolent Central Rule', *Washington Post*, 14 July, p A01.

United Nations Development Program. (2003) *Human Development Report*, New York: Oxford University Press.

Vasi, Ion Bogdan. (n.d.) 'From Global Justice to Domestic Anti-War: Social Movement Spillover and Mobilization', unpublished.

Väyrynen, Raimo. (2003) 'Regionalism: Old and New', *International Studies Review*, 5, No. 1 (March): 25–51.

The Violence against Women and War Network in Japan. Online. Available: <http://www1.jca.apc.org/vaww-net-japan/english/>

Walker, R. B. J. (1993) *Inside/Outside: International Relations as Political Theory*, Cambridge, UK: Cambridge University Press.

Wallach, Lori and Sforza, Michelle. (2000) *The WTO: Five Years of Reasons to Resist Corporate Globalization*, New York: Seven Stories Press.

Wallerstein, Immanuel. (2000) 'Globalization or the Age of Transition? A Long-Term View of the Trajectory of the World System', *International Sociology*, 15, No. 2: 249–65.

Walton, John and David Seddon. (1994) *Free Markets & Food Riots: The Politics of Global Adjustment*, Cambridge, MA: Blackwell.

Waltz, Kenneth N. (1979) *Theory of International Politics*, Reading, MA: Addison-Wesley.

—— (1999) 'Globalization and Governance', *Political Science & Politics: PS*, 32, No. 4 (December): 693–700.

Walzer, Michael. (1999) 'Rescuing Civil Society', *Dissent* (Winter): 62–7.

Wapner, Paul. (2002) 'Horizontal Politics: Transnational Environmental Activism and Global Cultural Change', *Global Environmental Politics*, 2, No. 2 (May): 37–62.

Watson, James L. (ed.) (1997). *Golden Arches East: McDonald's in East Asia*, Stanford, CA: Stanford University Press.

Weber, Max. (1949) '"Objectivity" in Social Science and Social Policy', in *The Methodology of the Social Sciences*, trans. and ed. Edward Shils and Henry A. Finch, New York: Free Press, 49–112.

——(1949) *The Methodology of the Social Sciences*, New York: Free Press.

——(1971) *From Max Weber: Essays in Sociology*, trans. and ed. H.H. Gerth and C. Wright Mills, New York: Oxford University Press.

——(1978) *Economy and Society: An Outline of Interpretive Sociology*, trans. Ephraim Fischoff *et al.* and ed. Guenther Roth and Claus Wittich, Berkeley: University of California Press.

Weiss, Linda. (1998) *The Myth of the Powerless State*, Ithaca, NY: Cornell University Press.

Wendt, Alexander. (1999) *Social Theory of International Politics*, Cambridge, UK: Cambridge University Press.

'The Women's Movement Then and Now', Special Issue, *AMPO: Japan–Asia Quarterly Review*, 25, No. 4, and 26, No. 1, 1995.

World Bank. (2000) *Globalization, Growth, and Poverty: Building an Inclusive World Economy*, Washington, DC: World Bank; New York: Oxford University Press.

Wrong, Dennis Hume. (1980) *Power, Its Forms, Bases and Uses*, New York: Harper and Row.

Wurm, Stephen A. (ed.) (1996) *Atlas of the World's Languages in Danger of Disappearing*, Paris: UNESCO.

Yasuda, Setsuko. (2000) 'Campaign against Genetically Modified Foods', *AMPO: Japan–Asia Quarterly Review*, 29, No. 2: 12–14.

Zeleza, Paul Tiyambe. (2003) *Rethinking Africa's Globalization*, Volume 1: *The Intellectual Challenges*, Trenton, NJ: Africa World Press.

Newspapers and periodicals (2000–2)

The Economist
Financial Times (London)
Guardian
Los Angeles Times
New Straits Times (Kuala Lumpur)
New York Times
Straits Times (Singapore)
Wall Street Journal
Washington Post
Washington Times

Name index

Subject index

In this index, **bold** type denotes text within tables.